A SEASON TO REMEMBER

LEEDS
1973-74

PUBLISHING
victorpublishing.co.uk

A SEASON TO REMEMBER

LEEDS
1973-74

A match by match account of Leeds' 1973/74 Football League title-winning season

with NEIL FISSLER

Introduction

NORMAN HUNTER maintained for many years before his death that it rankled him Don Revie isn't always mentioned in the same breath as some of the other great British managers of all time.

Revie is often forgotten when great managers are being discussed, falling behind the likes of Bill Shankly, Bob Paisley, Brian Clough and Jock Stein.

For a decade after leading Leeds to a Second Division title in 1964, the club enjoyed an unprecedented amount of success.

They won the League Championship twice, in 1969 and 1974. They also finished runners-up five times, won the Fairs Cup twice and were runners-up once.

They reached the Cup Winners Cup Final, the European Cup Final, and four FA Cup Finals, winning it once along with the League Cup.

But Leeds, under Revie, didn't win many friends, and it upset Hunter, who died in April 2020, that the manager doesn't get the credit he feels he deserves:

"Anybody from Yorkshire and Leeds United would think exactly the same. I didn't know any different than Don Revie. He came in and set the standards and set whatever we needed to do.

"And I never knew anything else other than success. It rankles me a little bit that he doesn't get mentioned up there with the very best managers.

"Alright, we had a bit of a reputation, and people didn't always like us, but that shouldn't take away from the fact that he was a great manager.

"We had total and utter respect. The minute he said something, nearly everybody agreed with him. Everything he told me to do, I did it without any questions asked.

"To me, he was a great manager. You couldn't approach him. He was the boss, but he would come and speak to you, and if it was a pat on the back, you appreciated that.

"He was ahead of his time in many, many ways, things like our diet and going away on a Friday night, which was unheard of at the time," he said.

Hunter pointed out that the success that the club enjoyed would have been even greater if they hadn't been challenging for trophies on so many fronts.

"We got involved in too many competitions, every year we were in the running for everything domestic and European, then one important game just rolled into another.

"The only time we won things quite easily was when we weren't involved in the league, so we said we will go and win the FA Cup.

"Another year, we were out of all of the competitions, so we said that we would go and win the league.

So I think we got involved in too many competitions.

"Also, not sour grapes, but there were one or two decisions that cost us dearly, they lost us two league titles."

There was little doubt about the destination of the Football League Championship trophy in 1973/74, with Revie's Leeds making a record-breaking start to the season...

MATCH 1 - 25 August 1973

LEEDS 3
EVERTON 1

Attendance: 39,425

MICK JONES was among the goals as Leeds eased themselves to an opening day victory at Elland Road. They only needed three minutes to open the scoring, Billy Bremner stumbled over an outstretched leg before regaining his balance and slamming past David Lawson. Peter Lorimer, Allan Clarke and Jones should have added to the score, while Clarke was the subject of savage tackling from Terry Darracott. Leeds doubled their lead after an hour, Johnny Giles lashing home into the bottom left-hand corner. Four minutes later, Bremner and Clarke paved the way for Jones to score from six yards. Everton, who were well beaten, pulled a 77th-minute goal back through Joe Harper.

LEEDS: David Harvey, Paul Reaney, Paul Madeley, Billy Bremner, Gordon McQueen, Norman Hunter, Peter Lorimer, Allan Clarke, Mick Jones, Johnny Giles, Eddie Gray

EVERTON: David Lawson, John McLaughlin, Terry Darracott, Mike Lyons, Roger Kenyon, Howard Kendall, Colin Harvey, Joe Harper, Joe Royle, Mick Buckley, John Connolly

Referee: JK Taylor

WHITES NEWS...

Leeds want George Best to come out of retirement to play in a testimonial for Billy Bremner. Best quit the game, saying he would never play again, but is wanted to play for Leeds against his former club, Manchester United, in a proposed game at Elland Road.

FIRST DIVISION HEADLINES...

Ray Kennedy, John Radford and Alan Ball are on target for Arsenal, who beat Man Utd 3-0... Doug Collins and Martin Dobson are on target in Burnley's 2-0 win at Sheffield Utd... Mick Coop scores for Coventry, who beat Spurs 1-0... Denis Law scored twice as Man City beat Birmingham 3-1.

FOOTBALL NEWS...

Alan Hudson admits he was "choked" after being dropped by Chelsea for the opening game at Derby... Derby boss Brian Clough fails in a bid to sign Bobby Moore, Trevor Brooking and Pop Robson from West Ham... Malcolm Allison, appearing on the Big Match, predicts Crystal Palace will win the Second Division title.

NEWS HEADLINES...

A man lost his hand in an explosion at the Bank of England, another went off on Oxford Street, and a warning stopped play at Lords for two hours... A letter bomb explodes at the US Embassy in Washington...Mortgage interest rates are expected to rise from 10 to 11 per cent.

UK's No 1 Single: Young Love - Donny Osmond

MATCH 2 - 28 August 1973

ARSENAL 1
LEEDS 2

Attendance: 47,273

PAUL MADELEY scored the winner as Leeds recovered from a disastrous start against The Gunners at Highbury. Arsenal needed just 65 seconds to go ahead when Jeff Blockley headed on John Radford's long throw, the ball bounced back off Mick Jones, and he scored from the rebound. England boss Sir Alf Ramsey and Scotland's Willie Ormond saw Peter Lorimer level with a 49th-minute free kick after Peter Storey left a gap in the wall. Eight minutes later, they got the winner when Johnny Giles wrestled the ball from Alan Ball in midfield before playing Madeley into space on the left, and his cross-shot cannoned in off Brockley.

ARSENAL: Bob Wilson, Pat Rice, Bob McNab, Peter Storey, Jeff Blockley, Peter Simpson (David Price), George Armstrong, Alan Ball, John Radford, Ray Kennedy, Charlie George

LEEDS David Harvey, Paul Reaney, Paul Madeley, Billy Bremner, Gordon McQueen, Norman Hunter, Peter Lorimer, Allan Clarke, Mick Jones, Johnny Giles, Eddie Gray

Referee: DRG Nippard

WHITES NEWS...

Terry Cooper took his first bath in two months after having a plaster cast taken off his left leg. Cooper underwent a bone graft operation in Manchester in the summer. Referee Jack Taylor, who handled the clash with Everton, hailed Leeds's new sporting attitude: "It was a highly entertaining game, because of the sporting behaviour."

FIRST DIVISION HEADLINES...

Frank Casper scores the only goal as Burnley beat Chelsea 1-0... Jim McCalliog and Derek Dougan are on target in Wolves' 2-0 win over Sheffield Utd... Martin Peters scores a brace as Spurs win 2-1 at Birmingham... Tommy Hutchison scores as Coventry beat Liverpool 1-0... Steve James earns Man Utd a 1-0 win over Stoke.

FOOTBALL NEWS...

Stoke agree to play a reserve game against Liverpool at 6.30 pm so Tommy Smith, who completes a two-match ban two hours earlier, can play... Terry Venables aims to silence the Tottenham boo boys after QPR drew their London rivals in the League Cup: "I feel I've got something to prove to Tottenham."

NEWS HEADLINES......

The IRA bomb three shops in Birmingham city Centre... A mini-sub laying cable 150 miles off the Cork coast is unable to surface... A BBC survey reveals 3.8m people have used cannabis at one time or another... 3000 men have been laid off at the Ford plant in Dagenham after a walkout by paint shop workers.

MATCH 3 - 1 September 1973

TOTTENHAM HOTSPUR 0
LEEDS 3

Attendance: 42,091

BILLY BREMNER scored twice as Leeds blew Spurs away with three goals in the first 28 minutes to maintain their 100 per cent start to the new season. Bremner, playing as an extra striker early on, headed home Peter Lorimer's fourth-minute free kick. Ten minutes later, Lorimer again caught out the Spurs' defence, and Bremner slammed a first-time shot off the post. He then laid on the third for Allan Clarke after 28 minutes with a low cross. Spurs fought back when Mike Dillon had two efforts blocked on the line by Paul Reaney and was denied by the bar before Alan Gilzean headed over from two yards.

TOTTENHAM: Pat Jennings, Ray Evans, Cyril Knowles, Ralph Coates, Mike Dillon, Phil Beal, Alan Gilzean, Steve Perryman, Martin Chivers, Martin Peters, Jimmy Neighbour

LEEDS David Harvey, Paul Reaney, Paul Madeley, Billy Bremner, Gordon McQueen, Norman Hunter, Peter Lorimer, Allan Clarke (Trevor Cherry), Mick Jones, Johnny Giles, Eddie Gray

Referee: RB Kirkpatrick

WHITES NEWS...

Allan Clarke had his knee put in plaster after being carried off against Tottenham, but it has been removed, and a specialist has examined it. Don Revie said: "The injury is a lot better than we thought it would be. At the moment, he has an outside chance of being able to play against Wolves."

FIRST DIVISION HEADLINES...

Second-placed Derby are held to a 0-0 draw at Birmingham... Martin Dobson's equaliser earns Burnley a 2-2 draw with Coventry... Bobby Stokes's last-minute winner sees Southampton beat Wolves 2-1... Sammy McIlroy's late winner helps Man Utd beat QPR 2-1.

FOOTBALL NEWS...

Sir Alf Ramsey is boosted by the Football League calling off First Division and League Cup matches around key World Cup qualifiers against Austria and Poland... Coventry, fearing midfielder Willie Carr will need a second cartilage operation in four months, send him to see his surgeon, who is on holiday in Scotland.

NEWS HEADLINES...

JRR Tolkien, who wrote The Hobbit and The Lord of the Rings, dies in Bournemouth aged 81... east end gangsters explode a bomb at West Ham police station in a revenge attack for police raids... The two-man crew of a mini-sub trapped for 77 hours on the bed of the Atlantic are reunited with their families.

MATCH 4 - 5 September 1973

LEEDS 4
WOLVERHAMPTON WANDERERS 1

Attendance: 39,946

PETER LORIMER scored a brace as Leeds put ten-man Wolves to the sword to continue their impressive start to the campaign. Wolves had Derek Parkin sent off after 78 minutes for flooring Eddie Gray with a mistimed tackle just eight minutes after being booked for a tackle on Lorimer. Leeds opened the scoring after three minutes. Phil Parkes pulled down Mick Jones, and Lorimer scored the resulting penalty. Mick Jones chipped a second in the 13th minute before Derek Dougan headed home after 30 minutes. Billy Bremner then squeezed a 50th-minute shot inside the post and ten minutes from time set up Lorimer to fire home the fourth.

LEEDS David Harvey, Paul Reaney, Paul Madeley, Billy Bremner, Gordon McQueen, Norman Hunter, Peter Lorimer, Allan Clarke, Mick Jones, Johnny Giles, Eddie Gray (Joe Jordan)

WOLVES: Phil Parkes, Gerry Taylor, Derek Parkin, Derek Jefferson (Jim McCalliog), Frank Munro, John McAlle, Barry Powell, Alan Sunderland, John Richards, Derek Dougan, Dave Wagstaffe

Referee: AWS Jones

WHITES NEWS...

Leeds boss Don Revie has spoken out in defence of under-fire England manager Sir Alf Ramsey: "The criticism Sir Alf Ramsey has had to take in recent months has been unbelievable. I believe they can go on and win the trophy (World Cup) again."

FIRST DIVISION HEADLINES...

Steve Kember, John Hollins and Ian Hutchinson are on target as Chelsea beat Birmingham 3-1... Frank Worthington's goal earns Leicester a 1-0 win over Man Utd... Rodney Marsh's penalty sees Man City beat Coventry 1-0... Late goals from Frank Casper and Doug Collins helped Burnley beat Spurs 3-2.

FOOTBALL NEWS...

Man Utd are ready to welcome back George Best after spending nine months in the football wilderness, and he could be fit to play in a month... The FA hold an emergency meeting to consider the criticism from Brian Clough in the Sunday Express and he could be asked to appear before a disciplinary committee.

NEWS HEADLINES...

The Queen has been advised not to visit Russia after an informal invitation given to Prince Philip... Career criminal Bertie Smalls claims he can keep £136,000 from 14 armed robberies in return for giving evidence against other criminals. The TUC vote to continue talking to the government about pay and prices...

MATCH 5 - 8 September 1973

LEEDS 3
BIRMINGHAM CITY 0

Attendance: 39,746

PETER LORIMER scored a hat-trick to take his tally to five goals in two games as rampant Leeds again went goal crazy and equalled their best run at the start of a season. He scored the first after 16 minutes, thumping home from 30 yards after Eddie Gray rolled a pass to him. Gray then headed against the bar before Lorimer added his second after 40 minutes from the penalty spot after Mick Jones was brought down. Seven minutes later, Gray ran 30 yards, passing inside to Lorimer, who drew Paul Cooper out of his goal before slipping the ball past him.

LEEDS David Harvey, Paul Reaney, Paul Madeley, Billy Bremner, Gordon McQueen, Norman Hunter, Peter Lorimer (Joe Jordan), Allan Clarke, Mick Jones, Johnny Giles, Eddie Gray

BIRMINGHAM: Paul Cooper, Ray Martin, Garry Pendrey, Malcolm Page, Roger Hynd, Kenny Burns, Jimmy Calderwood, Trevor Francis, Bob Latchford (Gordon Taylor), Steve Phillips, Bobby Hope

Referee: R Capey

WHITES NEWS...

Scotland boss Willie Ormond checked out several players ahead of the World Cup qualifier against Czechoslovakia. Peter Lorimer is unavailable because of suspension, and he feels Gray is short of match practice and needs a couple of games. Wolves are appealing Derek Parkin's sending-off against Leeds.

FIRST DIVISION HEADLINES...

Frank Casper and Geoff Nulty score as Burnley win 2-0 at Wolves... Kevin Keegan scores as Liverpool beat Chelsea 1-0... Mick Coop and Alan Green are on target as Coventry beat Southampton 2-0... Len Glover and Mike Stringfellow help Leicester win 2-0 at Arsenal.

FOOTBALL NEWS...

George Best resumes training with Manchester United after coming out of his self-imposed retirement: "I'm delighted to have George back," said boss Tommy Docherty... England World Cup winner Alan Ball claims referee Clive Thomas has a grudge against him after booking him for a fourth time in a defeat by Leicester.

NEWS HEADLINES...

Labour leader Harold Wilson is saved from drowning in the sea off the Isles of Scilly by Paul Wolff, a lifelong Tory voter... Bombs planted by the IRA, who have stepped up a London bombing campaign, are set off at Victoria, King's Cross and Euston stations in central London, injuring 13 people, three seriously.

MATCH 6 - 11 September 1973

WOLVERHAMPTON WANDERERS 0
LEEDS 2

Attendance: 36,980

MICK JONES and Allan Clarke secured Leeds a sixth successive win with goals in the opening 26 minutes as Don Revie's side equalled Arsenal's 1948 feat of winning their first six games. Jones opened the scoring after ten minutes when Phil Parkes, with one eye on Joe Jordan, slipped, and his shot rolled tamely into the net. They doubled their lead when Derek Jefferson tackled Billy Bremner, and the ball ran loose. Clarke, who was 25 yards out, fired in a dipping drive, leaving Parkes motionless. Wolves could have made it on an uncomfortable evening, but John Richards saw a header clip the top of the crossbar and Jim McCalliog also went close.

WOLVES: Phil Parkes, Gerry Taylor, Derek Parkin, Mike Bailey, Frank Munro, Derek Jefferson, Alan Sunderland (Steve Kindon), Jim McCalliog, John Richards, Derek Dougan, Steve Daley

LEEDS David Harvey, Trevor Cherry, Paul Madeley, Billy Bremner, Gordon McQueen, Norman Hunter, Terry Yorath, Allan Clarke, Mick Jones, Johnny Giles (Mick Bates), Joe Jordan

Referee: R Mathewson

WHITES NEWS...

Paul Reaney and Eddie Gray are set to recover from thigh injuries for the trip to Southampton. Johnny Giles faces a fitness test, but Peter Lorimer is out. The FA rejected a request for an independent assessor to report back on any booking after Don Revie discovered 70 per cent of their bookings were on away grounds.

FIRST DIVISION HEADLINES...

Ray Kennedy scores as Arsenal beat Sheffield Utd 1-0... Martin Peters is on target as Spurs draw 2-2 at Burnley... Rodney Marsh's last-minute strike can't prevent Man City losing 2-1 at Coventry... Derby County beat Liverpool 3-1... Alex Stepney scores a penalty, but Man Utd are defeated 2-1 by Leicester.

FOOTBALL NEWS...

Steve Burtenshaw quits as Arsenal's chief coach after 26 months following a fall-out with players, while Terry Venables has been appointed caretaker first-team coach by QPR... The FA say a clampdown on frivolous appeals by clubs attempting to get suspensions postponed is working. Only two players have appealed so far this season.

NEWS HEADLINES...

250,000 hospital workers and 60,000 London teachers could be among the those set for a pay boost the Pay Board has announced... The Government have given the green light for the digging of a Channel tunnel, which they hope to be completed by 1980 and open two years later.

MATCH 7 - 15 September 1973

SOUTHAMPTON 1
LEEDS 2

Attendance: 27,770

ALLAN CLARKE scored both goals as bookies made Don Revie's side 11-8 ON to become the Champions of England. Leeds edged nearer to Spurs's record of 11 successive wins when they won the double in 1961 with a seventh win on the spin. Mick Jones had a goal disallowed before Clarke opened the scoring with a 31st-minute volley after Eddie Gray found him with a chip. Leeds had to wait until the 76th minute to double their tally. Clarke stabbed home after Tony Bryne blocked his first effort. Southampton grabbed a last-minute consolation when Brian O'Neill lobbed David Harvey.

SOUTHAMPTON: Eric Martin, Bob McCarthy, Steve Mills, Hugh Fisher, Paul Bennett, Tony Byrne, Terry Paine, Wayne Talkes, Paul Gilchrist, Brian O'Neil, Bobby Stokes

LEEDS David Harvey, Paul Reaney, Paul Madeley, Billy Bremner, Gordon McQueen, Norman Hunter, Joe Jordan, Allan Clarke, Mick Jones, Paul Madeley, Eddie Gray

Referee: RC Challis

WHITES NEWS...

Allan Clarke is on target as Leeds are held 1-1 by Norwegian amateurs Stromsgodset IF in the UEFA Cup. Don Revie has earmarked cash to improve Elland Road: "We hope to have another good run in Europe. We need the money to go on improving our ground."

FIRST DIVISION HEADLINES...

Ray Hankin equalised to earn Burnley a 1-1 draw with Derby... Late goals from Irving Nattrass and Pat Howard see Newcastle beat Wolves 2-0... Alan Ball is among the scorers as Arsenal win 4-0 at Norwich... Brian Kidd scores twice in Man Utd's 3-1 win over West Ham.

FOOTBALL NEWS...

Bobby Moore has seen West Ham manager Ron Greenwood and told him he wants to leave his boyhood club, but the board refuse his demand... Ipswich could face UEFA action after Polish referee Stanislaw Eksztajn needed treatment when a missile stuck him in a 1-0 win over Real Madrid.

NEWS HEADLINES...

British Prime Minister Ted Heath flies to Dublin to meet Eire President Liam Cosgrove. It's the first official visit in 57 years, but talks fail... Mary Cairns, a nine-year Glasgow girl sentenced to 18 month's detention for stabbing a friend, has been given £1 bail pending an appeal.

MATCH 8 - 22 September 1973

LEEDS 0
MANCHESTER UNITED 0

Attendance: 47,058

LEEDS were denied an eighth successive win and now can't beat Spurs's record of 11 successive wins at the start of the season. However, Don Revie's side are three points clear of second placed Derby and have a game in hand. The visitors had the first chance when Jim Holton climbed above the defence to head over Kidd's free-kick. Leeds laid siege to their goal in the second half, but Allan Clarke couldn't reach Joe Jordan's pass. Jordan, Giles and Clarke had shots blocked as Leeds went looking for a winner before Jones's close-range shot cannoned off Alex Stepney to safety.

LEEDS David Harvey, Trevor Cherry, Paul Madeley, Billy Bremner, Gordon McQueen, Norman Hunter, Joe Jordan, Allan Clarke, Mick Jones, Johnny Giles, Eddie Gray

MAN UTD: Alex Stepney, Martin Buchan, Tony Young, Brian Greenhoff, Jim Holton, Steve James, Willie Morgan, Trevor Anderson, Lou Macari (George Buchan), Brian Kidd, George Graham

Referee: D Smith

WHITES NEWS...

Joe Jordan is the first Leeds player booked this season for an ill-tempered challenge on Brian Kidd. Don Revie ordered his players pre-season to clean up their act with a suspended £3,000 fine hanging over their heads. Leeds had 50 bookings last season, more than double the total for 1971-1972.

FIRST DIVISION HEADLINES...

Kevin Hector scores a hat-trick as Derby thrash Southampton 6-2... John Tudor's late equaliser earns Newcastle a 2-2 draw at Coventry... Chris Lawler gets a last-minute winner as Liverpool beat Spurs 3-2... Frank Worthington scores as Leicester draw 1-1 at West Ham.

FOOTBALL NEWS...

FA bosses have launched a TV advertising campaign to tempt crowds back to watch England after fans turn their back on Sir Alf Ramsey... Meanwhile Ramsey drops England captain Bobby Moore to face Austria after his failed bid to leave West Ham. England win 7-0, with Allan Clarke scoring twice.

NEWS HEADLINES...

Ted Heath dresses down Government advisor Lord Rothschild for claiming Britain will be one of the poorest countries in Europe by 1985... Traffic light maintenance workers in London go on strike in a row over pay. Families are facing an 11-week wait to get their holiday snaps back after a go-slow at Kodak's Hemel Hempstead factory.

UK's No 1 Single: Angel Fingers -Wizzard

MATCH 9 - 29 September 1973

NORWICH CITY 0
LEEDS 1

Attendance: 31,798

JOHNNY GILES scored the only goal as Leeds returned to winning ways to continue their unbeaten start to the season. But Essex referee Brian Daniels was the centre of attention after ruling out David Cross's stunning 13th-minute header for a push. Leeds broke from the free kick, and Giles's shot from 25 yards was helped into the net by Kevin Keelan. Norwich should have levelled, but Doug Livermore pushed a pass too far ahead of Colin Suggett, and David Harvey gathered. Duncan Forbes sent Joe Jordan tumbling in the area, but appeals for a penalty were rejected. Leeds hung on after the break, with Norwich's Ian Mellor going close.

NORWICH: Kevin Keelan, Colin Prophett, Les Wilson (Clive Payne), Dave Stringer, Duncan Forbes, Max Briggs, Doug Livermore, Colin Suggett, David Cross, Graham Paddon, Ian Mellor

LEEDS David Harvey, Paul Reaney, Trevor Cherry, Billy Bremner, Gordon McQueen, Norman Hunter, Joe Jordan, Allan Clarke, Mick Jones, Johnny Giles, Paul Madeley

Referee: BH Daniels

WHITES NEWS...

Ayr United goalkeeper David Stewart is signed for £30,000 while Gary Sprake, who had been interesting Man City, moves to Birmingham as Britain's most expensive 'keeper days after talks with Don Revie. Birmingham have also been watching Terry Yorath. Meanwhile, Revie has asked Celtic boss Jock Stein about Scotland international David Hay.

FIRST DIVISION HEADLINES...

Brian Anderson and Les Cartwright are on target as Coventry win 2-0 at Leicester... Paul Fletcher's brace helps Burnley beat Man City 3-2... Ralph Coates scores for Spurs, who beat Derby 1-0... John Tudor's late brace can't help Newcastle, who lose 3-2 to QPR... Man Utd draw 0-0 with Liverpool.

FOOTBALL NEWS...

ITV have offered £50,000 to show England's key World Cup clash with Poland live. They have already won the toss to show highlights... Man Utd boss Tommy Docherty warns rival clubs off making a bid for George Best: "We are not getting him fit for somebody else," he said.

NEWS HEADLINES...

Home Secretary Robert Carr has launched a crackdown on soft porn to make Britain look more decent, more appealing and less offensive... Shadow Chancellor Denis Healey unveils plans for a wealth tax and a new tax on luxury goods... Soaring food prices could see bacon rise by 4p a pound and eggs cost 9p each.

UK's No 1 Single: Eye Level - Simon Park Orchestra

MATCH 10 - 6 October 1973

LEEDS 1
STOKE CITY 1

Attendance: 36,553

MICK JONES scored his sixth goal of the season, but a late equaliser denied Leeds both points. Stoke had Geoff Hurst and John Mahoney booked in the opening two minutes before Johnny Giles had a goal disallowed for infringement on John Farmer. Leeds took the lead four minutes before half-time when John Farmer missed Allan Clarke's header, and Jones nodded into the empty goal. Leeds should have put the game out of reach, but Mick Bates struck the bar, and Farmer twice denied Peter Lorimer. Stoke made them pay in the last minute when their biggest threat, Terry Conroy, ghosted past Trevor Cherry and Bates before centring for Denis Smith to equalise.

LEEDS David Harvey, Paul Reaney, Trevor Cherry, Billy Bremner, Paul Madeley, Norman Hunter, Peter Lorimer (Terry Yorath), Allan Clarke, Mick Jones, Johnny Giles, Mick Bates

STOKE: John Farmer, Jackie Marsh, Mike Pejic, John Mahoney, Denis Smith, Alan Dodd, Terry Conroe, Jimmy Greenhoff, Geoff Hurst, Dave Goodwin (Terry Lees), Sean Haslegrave

Referee: M Sinclair

WHITES NEWS...

Norman Hunter makes his 600th appearance in the 2-0 League Cup defeat at Ipswich Town. Don Revie warns next year's World Cup could be a bloodbath unless referees are stronger and FIFA lays down strict rules. Norwegian amateurs Stromsgodset IF are beaten 6-1 in the UEFA Cup at Elland Road.

FIRST DIVISION HEADLINES...

Colin Waldron scores as Burnley win 1-0 at West Ham... Late goals from Mike Lyons and John Connolly see Everton win 2-1 at Coventry... Roger Davies is on target as Derby draw 1-1 with Norwich... Alec Lindsay's late penalty helps Liverpool beat Newcastle 2-1.

FOOTBALL NEWS...

Two Thousand police are on duty as Argentina beat Paraguay to qualify for the World Cup finals... Sir Alf Ramsey flies to Rotterdam to watch World Cup opponents Poland in action against Holland... Harry Johnston, who led Blackpool to victory in the 1953 FA Cup "Matthews Final," dies in Blackpool aged 54.

NEWS HEADLINES...

Elvis Presley is set to pay wife Priscilla millions of dollars as part of a divorce settlement ... Chancellor Anthony Barber brands Enoch Powell a 'frustrated fanatic' in a ferocious party conference speech... Spiro Agnew resigns as US Vice-President after pleading guilty to tax fraud.

MATCH 11 - 13 October 1973

LEICESTER CITY 2
LEEDS 2

Attendance: 36,978

BILLY BREMNER'S equaliser saw Leeds come back from two goals down to earn a seventh draw in their last nine trips to Filbert Street. They are, however, still looking for their first win at the ground. They fell behind in the 10th minute after Frank Worthington was given a generous amount of space to crack home a half-volley. Nine minutes later, Alan Birchenall hammered home a 30-yard rocket, but Leeds fought back. Mick Jones prodded home a Peter Lorimer pass after 23 minutes, and five minutes before the break, Johnny Giles pushed a cheeky quick free-kick through to Bremner to score.

LEICESTER: Peter Shilton, Steve Whitworth, Dennis Rolfe, Mike Stringfellow, Malcolm Munro, Alan Woollett, Keith Weller, Jon Sammels, Frank Worthington, Alan Birchenall, Len Glover

LEEDS David Harvey, Trevor Cherry, Paul Madeley, Billy Bremner, Gordon McQueen, Norman Hunter, Peter Lorimer, Allan Clarke, Mick Jones, Johnny Giles (Joe Jordan), Mick Bates

Referee: AL Hart

WHITES NEWS...

Eddie Gray is out for three or four weeks with a thigh injury: "Eddie has had some terrible luck with injuries, but this is only a minor operation, and he should be playing again in three to four weeks," said boss Don Revie. Billy Bremner misses Scotland's World Cup qualifier with Czechoslovakia.

FIRST DIVISION HEADLINES...

Ray Hankin scores Burnley's winner in a 2-1 victory over QPR... Late goals from Alan Gilzean and Martin Chivers see Spurs beat Arsenal 2-0... Kevin Hector's winner helps Derby see off Man Utd 1-0... Coventry draw 0-0 at Norwich... Mick Channon's penalty earns Southampton a 1-0 win over Liverpool.

FOOTBALL NEWS...

Derby accept the resignations of manager Brian Clough and his assistant Peter Taylor. Derby claims Clough broke his contract with TV appearances and newspaper articles... Clough then calls Poland goalkeeper Jan Tomaszewski "a clown" on TV as England crash out of the World Cup with a 1-1 draw at Wembley.

NEWS HEADLINES...

Petrol is set to rise by 2p a gallon to 40p after Gulf states put up crude oil by 17 per cent... Israeli forces cross the Suez Canal on a hit-and-run mission on Egyptian missile sites... The Government face a mini general election with four by-elections in Hove, Berwick, Edinburgh North and Goven on November 8.

MATCH 12 - 20 October 1973

LEEDS 1
LIVERPOOL 0

Attendance: 44,901

MICK JONES was again the Leeds-scoring hero, as his first-half strike was enough to see off Liverpool. Don Revie's side will feel, however, they should have won by more than one goal. Ray Clemence denied Mick Jones after five minutes following Peter Lorimer's inspired through ball. Kevin Keegan missed a chance to break the deadlock, and Leeds made them pay. Lorimer bent a 25th-minute cross around John Toshack, and Jones headed just under the bar. Lorimer finished off a six man move by thumping just wide, then in the second half, Bremner blasted wide with the route to goal left gaping after Peter Cormack slipped.

LEEDS David Harvey, Paul Madeley, Trevor Cherry, Billy Bremner, Gordon McQueen, Norman Hunter, Peter Lorimer, Allan Clarke, Mick Jones, Johnny Giles, Mick Bates, Terry Yorath

LIVERPOOL: Ray Clemence, Chris Lawler, Alec Lindsay, Tommy Smith, Larry Lloyd,

Emlyn Hughes, Kevin Keegan, Peter Cormack, Steve Highway, John Toshack, Ian Callaghan

Referee: PJ Richardson

WHITES NEWS...

Don Revie is set to use the club's floodlight pylons with a full, unobstructed view of the pitch in a videotaping experiment and believes that, eventually, clubs will employ full-time doctors. Leeds and England trainer Les Cocker will act as Sponge Man when he helps out Republic of Ireland boss Johnny Giles for the World Cup qualifier against Poland.

FIRST DIVISION HEADLINES...

Dave Clements scores a penalty as Everton overcome Burnley 1-0... John McGovern scores as managerless Derby beat Leicester 2-1... Malcolm McDonald gets a brace as Newcastle beat Chelsea 2-0... John McDowell gets the only goal for West Ham, who beat Coventry 1-0.

FOOTBALL NEWS...

George Best returns to league action after a year out, playing 77 minutes in Man Utd's 1-0 win over Birmingham... Derby County name Dave Mackay as manager in succession to Brian Clough despite player pleas for his reinstatement... A retired businessman offers Nottingham Forest £90,000 over five years to cover Clough and Peter Taylor's wages.

NEWS HEADLINES...

President Nixon backs down and hands over his White House tape recordings on the Watergate scandal... Thousands of callers jam BBC phone lines after being invited to put questions to Prime Minister Edward Heath on TV... Trade and Industry minister Peter Walker rules out petrol rationing but urged motorists to travel by bus or car.

MATCH 13 - 27 October 1973

MANCHESTER CITY 0
LEEDS 1

Attendance: 45,363

MICK BATES scored the only goal, but Leeds found City a tough nut to crack before clocking up a sixth away win out of seven. City could have gone ahead, but Alan Oakes badly sliced wide and claims for a penalty after Paul Madeley handled Tony Towers's shot were waved away. Early in the second half, Gordon McQueen lost control, and City carved open a chance for Towers to badly miscue. Mick Jones fired over the bar when clean through after an hour before the only goal arrived after 76 minutes when Tommy Booth headed out to Bates, who slammed a first-time shot past Keith MacRae from the edge of the box.

MAN CITY: Keith MacRae, Glyn Pardoe, Willie Donachie, Mike Doyle, Tommy Booth, Alan Oakes, Mike Summerbee, Colin Bell, Denis Law (Dennis Leman), Francis Lee, Tony Towers

LEEDS David Harvey, Trevor Cherry, Paul Madeley, Billy Bremner, Gordon McQueen, Norman Hunter, Peter Lorimer, Allan Clarke, Mick Jones, Johnny Giles (Joe Jordan), Mick Bates

Referee: IP Jones

WHITES NEWS...

Gordon McQueen is told that his yellow card in Billy Bremner's testimonial at Stirling Albion will count against him. McQueen was booked for a foul in the 3-2 win in front of Jock Stein and Willie Ormond. Mick Bates scored two and Mick Bates the other.

FIRST DIVISION HEADLINES...

Joe Harper and John Connolly score as Everton beat Birmingham 2-0... Burnley are held 0-0 by Man Utd... Derby draw 0-0 at West Ham... Stewart Barrowclough and Tommy Gibb score as Newcastle win 2-0 at Spurs... Kevin Keegan scores for Liverpool, who beat Sheffield Utd 1-0.

FOOTBALL NEWS...

Brian Clough becomes Brighton's manager on £12,000 a year with Peter Taylor, his £8,000 assistant... Frank O'Farrell accepts £45,000 after being sacked by Manchester United in an out-of-court settlement... Martin Chivers has showdown talks with Spurs boss Bill Nicolson after Man City rejected swapping him with Rodney Marsh.

NEWS HEADLINES...

Strikes by fireman over pay in Glasgow spread to Essex, Bristol and London. They have rejected £2.48 an hour... A Roman Catholic priest, Patrick Fell, is jailed for 12 years for recruiting an IRA cell from his Coventry congregation... Britain faces power cuts because of an overtime ban by engineers.

UK's No 1 Single: Daydreamer/Puppy Dog - David Cassidy

MATCH 14 - 3 November 1973

LEEDS 4
WEST HAM UNITED 1

Attendance: 35,869

MICK JONES was on target twice as Leeds turned the screw on struggling West Ham to retain six points clear at the top of the table. The result was never in doubt once Mick Bates accepted the rebound from his own 19th-minute shot for his fourth goal in three matches. Two minutes later, Jones nipped in between John McDowell and Frank Lampard for the second. He punished hesitation between Alan Taylor and Mervyn Day for the third after 51 minutes. Allan Clarke rose above the defence to score the fourth after 57 minutes from Bates's cross before West Ham pulled a goal back eight minutes from time when Ted MacDougall headed past David Harvey.

LEEDS David Harvey, Paul Reaney, Trevor Cherry, Billy Bremner, Gordon McQueen, Norman Hunter, Peter Lorimer, Allan Clarke, Mick Jones, Mick Bates, Paul Madeley

WEST HAM: Mervyn Day, Keith Coleman, Frank Lampard, Billy Bonds, Tommy Taylor, Bobby Moore, Dudley Tyler, John McDowell, Clyde Best, Trevor Brooking, Ted MacDougall

Referee: J Williams

WHITES NEWS...

Don Revie is still interested in Celtic's Scotland international David Hay. Ron Revie booked a £7.50 a night room at an Edinburgh hotel for the team's baggage before his side beat Hibs 5-4 on penalties in the UEFA Cup after a second 0-0 draw.

FIRST DIVISION HEADLINES...

Dennis Rofe scores in his own goal as Leicester lose 1-0 at Norwich... Tommy Gibb gets the winner as Newcastle beat Stoke 2-1... Steve Perryman earns Spurs a 1-1 draw at Everton... Stan Bowles scores as QPR beat Derby 2-1... Tony Young and Brian Greenhoff help Man Utd draw 2-2 with Chelsea.

FOOTBALL NEWS...

Chancellor Anthony Barber could be asked for £1,000,000 to modernise football terraces after 66 died in the Ibrox Disaster in 1971... Tommy Smith could retire after being left out of the game at Arsenal and making his own way home... Northern Ireland recall George Best after just 255 minutes of First Division action.

NEWS HEADLINES...

American President Nixon is refusing to quit over the Watergate scandal... US Secretary of State Dr Henry Kissinger claims to be moving towards peace in the Middle East after talks with Egypt's President Sadat... Liberals candidate Alan Beith wins the Berwick-on-Tweed by-election by just 57 votes from the Tories.

MATCH 15 - 10 November 1973

BURNLEY 0
LEEDS 0

Attendance: 40,087

ALLAN CLARKE missed a late-minute chance as Leeds extended their unbeaten run to 15 games in a fascinating top-of-the-table dual. Clarke, who had cleared the crossbar with the first chance of the game after three minutes, rattled the woodwork with a 12-yard shot with almost the last kick. Leeds were the better team in the opening period and should have scored when Clarke crashed a 23rd-minute shot against Alan Stevenson's bar, and Peter Lorimer fired the rebound over. Leeds engineered very little after the break, while David Harvey was kept busy as the Clarets sought to break the deadlock.

BURNLEY: Alan Stevenson, Peter Noble, Keith Newton, Martin Dobson, Colin Waldron, Jim Thomson, Geoff Nulty, Ray Hankin (Billy Ingham), Paul Fletcher, Doug Collins, Leighton James

LEEDS David Harvey, Paul Reaney, Trevor Cherry, Billy Bremner, Gordon McQueen, Norman Hunter, Peter Lorimer, Allan Clarke, Mick Jones, Mick Bates (Joe Jordan), Paul Madeley

Referee: JH Yates

WHITES NEWS...

Johnny Giles has been told to rest for a fortnight before seeing a special who will decide whether or not to operate on a long-standing calf injury. Giles has missed ten of the last 15 matches. Norman Hunter is expected to recover from a groin injury for the trip to Coventry City.

FIRST DIVISION HEADLINES...

Keith Weller scores as Leicester beat Newcastle 1-0... Steve Highway is on target in Liverpool's 1-0 win over Wolves... Peter Osgood nets twice in Chelsea's 3-1 win over Everton... Mick Lambert's brace helps Ipswich secure a 3-0 win over Derby.

FOOTBALL NEWS...

Football League secretary Alan Hardaker says any player signing up to the travelling Soccer Circus would be breaking his contract... Bobby Moore is staying with West Ham until the end of the season after talks with Ron Greenwood... League Cup fourth-round ties next week have been switched from evening to 2.15 kick-offs because of the power crisis.

NEWS HEADLINES...

A dispute by power engineers moves into a second week, threatening power cuts... Princess Anne marries Captain Mark Phillips in Westminster Abbey... Esso announce they are imposing petrol rationing after the war in the Middle East hits supplies... The IRA are threatening revenge attacks after eight terrorists were jailed for life in London...

MATCH 16 - 17 November 1973

LEEDS 3
COVENTRY CITY 0

Attendance: 35,522

JOE JORDAN scored his first goal of the season to help Leeds stay seven points clear of the chasing pack. Don Revie's side opened the scoring after nine minutes when Allan Clarke received the ball just inside the Coventry half before beating Bill Glazier from 20 yards. Billy Bremner was upset to be denied a 25th-minute penalty when Alen Dugdale tripped him, and the second goal didn't arrive until the 69th minute. Gordon McQueen burst through the middle and Bremner flicked to Mick Bates, whose cross was headed home by Jordan. Five minutes later, Norman Hunter pulled the ball back from the byline, and Bremner rounded off the scoring with a first-time shot.

LEEDS David Harvey, Paul Reaney, Trevor Cherry, Billy Bremner, Gordon McQueen, Norman Hunter, Peter Lorimer (Terry Yorath), Allan Clarke, Joe Jordan, Mick Bates, Paul Madeley

COVENTRY: Bill Glazier, Mick Coop, Jimmy Holmes, Dennis Mortimer (Les Cartwright), Bobby Parker, Alan Dugdale, David Cross, Brian Alderson, Colin Stein, Mick McGuire, Tommy Hutchison

Referee: AE Morrissey

WHITES NEWS...

Don Revie is banned from the touchline and dressing room for the first leg of UEFA Cup against Vitoria Setubal. Hibs protested after Revie had stayed on the pitch during the penalty shoot-out win at Easter Road. Les Cocker is censured for entering the field of play without permission. Paul Madeley is battling a knee injury.

FIRST DIVISION HEADLINES...

George Hope scores the winner as Newcastle beat Man Utd 3-2... Kevin Keegan scores a hat-trick in Liverpool's 4-2 win over Ipswich... Everton win 3-1 at Norwich City, with Mike Bernard among the scorers... Burnley lose 2-0 at Leicester thanks to goals from Len Glover and Mike Stringfellow.

FOOTBALL NEWS...

Dagenham will train in the club car park with light being provided by their players' cars... Derby players break their contracts and refuse to train under new boss Dave Mackay before 90-minute peace talks....Ron Saunders is appointed Man City boss, five days after resigning from Norwich City on a four-year contract worth £50,000...

NEWS HEADLINES...

The Government has ordered a 10 per cent cut in oil supplies, and motorists are asked not to drive on Sundays... They are braced for an uncomfortable winter after miners' leaders reject the latest pay offer... Kidnappers send pictures to an Italian newspaper showing Paul Getty missing an ear as they step up demands for £1m ransom.

UK's No 1 Single: I Love You Love Me Love - Gary Glitter

MATCH 17 - 24 November 1973

DERBY COUNTY 0
LEEDS 0

Attendance: 36,003

LEEDS edged closer to Liverpool's post-war record after drawing a game with more bookings than shots on target. Don Revie's side, who are unbeaten in 17 matches - two short of Liverpool's 19 game post-war record - had Gordon McQueen and Billy Bremner booked by referee Harry New, while Derby also picked up a brace of bookings. Derby players, who have been in turmoil, threatening to strike after Brian Clough left, could have taken the lead in the first minute through Alan Hinton. The nearest Leeds came was through Joe Jordan, shooting straight at Colin Boulton, while Derby's Archie Gemmill miskicked when presented with an open goal.

DERBY: Colin Boulton, Ron Webster, David Nish, Henry Newton, Roy McFarland, Colin Todd, John McGovern, Archie Gemmill, John O'Hare (Roger Davies), Kevin Hector, Alan Hinton

LEEDS David Harvey, Paul Reaney, Trevor Cherry, Billy Bremner, Gordon McQueen, Norman Hunter, Peter Lorimer, Allan Clarke, Joe Jordan, Mick Bates, Terry Yorath

Referee: H New

WHITES NEWS...

The Scottish FA have turned down a request for their World Cup squad to play Leeds in a testimonial match for Billy Bremner. The Scottish FA stated that it is their policy after they turned down a request from Celtic for a game for Billy McNeil. Leeds beat Vitoria 1-0 in the UEFA Cup, with Trevor Cherry scoring.

FIRST DIVISION HEADLINES...

Mike Lyons scores for Everton, who draw 1-1 with Newcastle... Paul Fletcher scores as Burnley beat Stoke 1-0... Frank McLintock gets a late equaliser for QPR, who draw 2-2 with Liverpool... Alan Ball's brace helps Arsenal beat West Ham 3-1.

FOOTBALL NEWS...

The FA orders a full investigation of the game from park football to the England team... The Football League order all afternoon matches to kick off at 2pm during the electricity crisis... Jack Charlton is sending striker Alan Foggon to his mother Cissie's Carlton Moors farmhouse to lose 7lbs to increase his pace.

NEWS HEADLINES...

Petrol rationing books are set to be issued next week Trade Secretary Peter Walker tells the Commons... Enoch Powell questions Prime Minster Ted Heath's state of mind in a speech to a London lunch... Labour will thrash out a policy programme in case Mr Heath decides to call a snap election.

MATCH 18 - 1 December 1973

LEEDS 2
QUEENS PARK RANGERS 2

Attendance: 32,194

BILLY BREMNER and Mick Jones were on target, but a late Stan Bowles equaliser denied Leeds a 13th win of the season. They did, however, move to within a game of Liverpool's 19-game unbeaten record. Rangers opened the scoring after 35 minutes when Don Givens controlled Terry Venables's free-kick before scoring. Leeds levelled after 47 minutes. Mick Jones's long ball found Bremner, who shot wide of Phil Parkes. Five minutes later, Terry Yorath chipped the ball over the defence. Jones let the ball bounce before firing home. Joe Jordan headed over from six yards before Bowles nipped in to beat Harvey from just inside the area after 82 minutes to snatch a point.

LEEDS David Harvey, Paul Reaney, Trevor Cherry, Billy Bremner, Gordon McQueen, Norman Hunter, Peter Lorimer, Allan Clarke, Mick Jones, Mick Bates (Joe Jordan, Terry Yorath

QPR: Phil Parkes, Dave Clement, Tony Hazell, Terry Venables, Terry Mancini, Frank McLintock, Dave Thomas, Gerry Francis, Mick Leach, Stan Bowles, Don Givens

Referee: RB Lee

WHITES NEWS...

Allan Clarke is out of the UEFA Cup third-round tie against Vitoria Setubal in Portugal after being booked in both legs of the win over Hibs, the club has been told in a cable from UEFA. Don Revie has sounded a warning ahead of their next league match at Portman Road: "Ipswich are the biggest hurdle we have yet faced."

FIRST DIVISION HEADLINES...

Sammy Nelson equalises to earn Arsenal a 2-2 draw with Coventry... Len Glover scores twice as Coventry City beat Spurs 3-0. Steve Earle is also on target... Mick Channon scores a late penalty as Southampton beat Everton 2-0... Peter McCormack scores for Liverpool, who beat West Ham 1-0.

FOOTBALL NEWS...

Arsenal are fined £2,000 after admitting an illegal approach to QPR duo Gerry Francis and Phil Parkes... Brian Clough has been given a vote of confidence from Brighton and Hove after an 8-2 hammering by Bristol Rovers... Ted MacDougall becomes the first player in history to cost £500,000 in transfer fees after joining Norwich from West Ham for £130,000.

NEWS HEADLINES...

ASLEF bans all overtime after rejecting a 12 per cent pay off from British Rail... Petrol pumps run dry after panic buying, with MPs from all sides calling for rationing to be implemented as soon as possible... The Stock Exchange suffers its worst-ever crash after the FT index slumped by 19.7 points, costing £2,000m.

MATCH 19 - 8 December 1973

IPSWICH TOWN 0
LEEDS 3
Attendance: 27,313

ALLAN CLARKE scored the 100th goal of his career as Leeds equalled Liverpool's 24-year-old post-World War Two record of 19 games unbeaten. Clarke rounded off a clinical display from Leeds with a right-foot finish to an 87th-minute weaving run. Ipswich, who knocked Leeds out of the League Cup, were only level at half-time thanks to goalkeeper David Best. He was finally beaten six minutes after the break when Terry Yorath's lob deflected off Allan Hunter. Yorath was the provider for the second goal after 58 minutes when Mick Jones's header from his centre gave Best no chance.

LEEDS David Harvey, Paul Reaney, Trevor Cherry, Billy Bremner, Gordon McQueen, Norman Hunter, Peter Lorimer, Allan Clarke (Joe Jordan), Mick Jones, Terry Yorath, Paul Madeley

IPSWICH: David Best, Geoff Hammond, Mick Mills, Peter Morris (Bryan Hamilton), Allan Hunter, Kevin Beattie, Ian Collard, Colin Viljoen, David Johnson, Trevor Whymark, Clive Woods

Referee: JK Taylor

WHITES NEWS...

Don Revie is counting the cost of the win at Ipswich following injuries to Peter Lorimer (knee), Trevor Cherry (thigh), David Harvey (swollen eye) and Gordon McQueen (groin). Clarke is ruled out of the trip to Chelsea with a virus. Leeds crashed out of the UEFA Cup after being beaten 3-1 in Portugal by Vitoria Setubal.

FIRST DIVISION HEADLINES...

Alan Waddle scores as Liverpool win the Merseyside derby with Everton 1-0... Billy Ingham scores in Burnley's 1-0 win over Norwich... Newcastle lose 1-0 at Birmingham, with Kenny Burns scoring... QPR draw 0-0 with Sheffield Utd. Mike Doyle's own goal costs Man City, who lost 2-1 at West Ham.

FOOTBALL NEWS...

Wolves invite nine other Midland clubs to a meeting to lobby for a month's suspension to the season during the fuel crisis... Glentoran want to bring Jimmy Greaves out of retirement to help with their bid for Cup Winners Cup glory... Derby's Welsh international defender Terry Hennessey is set to be forced into retirement after nine months out with an ankle injury.

NEWS HEADLINES...

London faces a teacher crisis with 1,000 set to quit at Christmas because they can't afford to live in the capital... BBC TV and Independent TV will close down no later than 10.30 to save Christmas as electricity supplies are limited... A three day week for shops, offices and factories has been announced from January 1st as the power crisis bites.

MATCH 20 - 15 December 1973

CHELSEA 1
LEEDS 2

Attendance: 40,768

MICK JONES scored the goal that broke Liverpool's post-World War Two record 19-game unbeaten start to the season. Leeds survived an early scare when, after only 30 seconds, Trevor Cherry's slip gave Steve Kember a free shot, which David Harvey stopped. Leeds opened the scoring a minute before the break when Jordan kept his nerve after a strong challenge on Peter Bonetti by Jones. Chelsea levelled after 54 minutes when Peter Houseman's inswinging corner was headed home by Peter Osgood. But they couldn't build on it, and after 68 minutes, Jordan unselfishly headed Peter Lorimer's centre back to Jones to score the record-breaking winner.

CHELSEA: Peter Bonetti, Gary Locke, Ron Harris, John Hollins, Dave Webb, Steve Kember, Chris Garland, Tommy Baldwin, Peter Osgood, Alan Hudson, Peter Houseman

LEEDS David Harvey, Paul Reaney, Trevor Cherry, Billy Bremner, Gordon McQueen, Norman Hunter, Peter Lorimer, Joe Jordan, Mick Jones, Terry Yorath, Paul Madeley

Referee: DJ Biddle

WHITES NEWS...

Don Revie praised his players after setting a 20-game unbeaten record: "The players are the ones who created this record of 20 league matches without defeat, and they are the ones who should take the credit. I am very happy that they have managed to achieve it in style."

FIRST DIVISION HEADLINES...

Paul Cheesley scores for Norwich, who hold Liverpool 1-1... Colin Waldron scores the winner for Burnley, who beat Arsenal 2-1... Dave Clements levels for Everton, held to a 1-1 draw by Sheffield Utd... David Cross's winner sees Coventry beat Man Utd 3-2. Wolves beat Stoke 3-2.

FOOTBALL NEWS...

The Football League rules out a month-long break, saying it would cost them £250,000... The FA have asked for special dispensation to waive the Sunday Observance Act to allow Sunday football during the power crisis... Spurs are trying to lure back thousands of stay-away fans with 11.15 kick-offs but admit it's a gamble.

NEWS HEADLINES...

The Royal Mail say they cannot guarantee Christmas post deliveries because of the rail dispute... The IRA explode a car bomb in Westminster, which leaves 54 in hospital... Prime Minister Ted Heath holds peace talks with six top TUC men amid talk of a general strike... Seven people are killed when a packed rush hour train jumps rails in Ealing, West London.

UK's No 1 Single: Merry Xmas Everybody - Slade

MATCH 21 - 22 December 1973

LEEDS 1
NORWICH CITY 0

Attendance: 34,747

TERRY YORATH scored the only goal as Leeds continued their unbeaten start to the season. His well-placed 56th-minute header from the edge of the area from Peter Lorimer's free kick finally broke The Canaries' stubborn resistance. Until then, it looked like Kevin Keelan would stop everything thrown his way, denying Paul Reaney, Mick Jones, Lorimer and Joe Jordan on Billy Bremner's 500th appearance for the First Division leaders. Norwich, without an away win all season, attempted without any luck to muster an effort on goal in the second half despite the industry of Colin Suggett and Paul Cheesley.

LEEDS David Harvey, Paul Reaney, Trevor Cherry, Billy Bremner, Gordon McQueen, Norman Hunter, Peter Lorimer, Joe Jordan, Mick Jones, Terry Yorath, Paul Madeley

NORWICH: Kevin Keelan, Mel Machin, Colin Prophett, Dave Stringer, Duncan Forbes, Trevor Howard, Steve Grapes, Ted MacDougall, Colin Suggett, Paul Cheesley (Neil O'Donnell), Max Briggs

Referee: D Turner

WHITES NEWS...

Don Revie will take a squad of 14 to the north east for the Boxing Day clash with Newcastle. Billy Bremner (ankle) and Terry Yorath (also ankle) will be given fitness tests on the morning of the game. Leeds aim to equal Sheffield United's 1899-1900 record of a 22 game unbeaten start to a season.

FIRST DIVISION HEADLINES...

Kevin Keegan and Steve Highway score as Liverpool beat Man Utd 2-0... Burnley lose ground after being defeated 2-0 at Man City... Alan Hinton gets both goals in Derby's 2-0 win over Spurs... Stan Bowles's last-minute winner helps QPR beat Newcastle 3-2.

FOOTBALL NEWS...

Every woman going to QPR v Newcastle will be entered into a raffle to win one of four 12lbs turkeys... The FA have given the green light for Sunday football for the first time - admission will be by inflated programme price... Arsenal's Alan Ball upsets rivals Spurs by suggesting on the Big Match they could get relegated.

NEWS HEADLINES...

Three bombs explode in London's Theatreland without warning as the IRA step up a Christmas bombing campaign...A policeman and two other people are shot dead by a gunman in Torquay, Devon... Prime Minister Ted Heath is locked in a battle with unions insisting the three day week won't be lifted until coal supplies are flowing again.

MATCH 22 - 26 December 1973

NEWCASTLE UNITED 0
LEEDS 1

Attendance: 54,475

PAUL MADELEY scored his second goal of the season to keep Leeds nine points clear at the top of the table. Madeley, whose other goal came at Arsenal in August, scored a 30-yard beauty following Peter Lorimer's 29th-minute pass. The estimated 10,000 locked out, a record crowd for the newly constructed St James Park, missed Leeds winning their sixteenth game in 22. Leeds were lucky that Malcolm McDonald wasn't at his sharpest on his return from injury, with David Harvey keeping him and John Tudor at bay with superb second half saves when they played possession football and stroked the ball around.

NEWCASTLE: Willie McFaul, David Craig, Frank Clark, Terry McDermott, Pat Howard, Bobby Moncur, Tommy Gibb, Jim Smith (Tommy Cassidy), Malcolm McDonald, John Tudor, Terry Hibbitt

LEEDS David Harvey, Paul Reaney, Trevor Cherry, Billy Bremner, Gordon McQueen, Norman Hunter, Peter Lorimer, Joe Jordan, Mick Jones, Terry Yorath, Paul Madeley

Referee: H Davey

WHITES NEWS...

Gordon McQueen has a groin injury, and Joe Jordan has an ankle problem so both will have fitness tests ahead of the visit to Birmingham City. Allan Clarke still isn't over a knee injury, while Freddie Goodwin, former Leeds star now in charge at St Andrew's, says: "They have no apparent weakness, but they're not unbeatable."

FIRST DIVISION HEADLINES...

Ray Hankin scores the winner for Burnley, who beat Liverpool 2-1... John Hurst and Mick Buckley score for Everton, who beat Man City 2-0... Derby are held 0-0 at Stoke, Spurs and QPR also draw 0-0... Clyde Best gets two in West Ham's 4-2 win at Chelsea.

FOOTBALL NEWS...

Bolton and Stoke make history when they announce their FA Cup third round tie will be played on Sunday, January 6th... Brighton boss Brian Clough has gagged himself after only one win in ten since moving to the South Coast... Russia could be reinstated to the World Cup despite failing to play Chile in the second leg of a play-off.

NEWS HEADLINES...

Miners union boss Joe Gormley has blamed the Coal Board for a lack of urgency after four hours of emergency talks... The Queen is planning to spend £250,000 modernising Sandringham House... 400,000 workers in North-West England and the Midlands have been laid off because of government-enforced power restrictions.

MATCH 23 - 29 December 1973

BIRMINGHAM CITY 1
LEEDS 1

Attendance: 50,451

JOE JORDAN's 88th-minute equaliser wrote Leeds place in the history books with a record-breaking run of going unbeaten in their opening 23 games. Jordan snatched a draw from the jaws of defeat when he hammered home a Peter Lorimer cross. The Scottish international, who was only playing after passing a late fitness test, had earlier had a goal disallowed for offside. Birmingham took the lead after 21 minutes when Bob Latchford steered Alan Campbell's pass past David Harvey. It looked to be enough, and Jordan's leveller came two minutes after Latchford had a second goal chalked off for an infringement.

BIRMINGHAM: Gary Sparke, Ray Martin, Joe Gallagher, Garry Pendrey, John Roberts, Kenny Burns, Alan Campbell, Trevor Francis, Bob Latchford, Bob Hatton, Gordon Taylor

LEEDS David Harvey, Paul Reaney, Trevor Cherry, Billy Bremner, Gordon McQueen, Norman Hunter, Peter Lorimer, Joe Jordan, Mick Jones, Terry Yorath, Paul Madeley

Referee: IT Smith

WHITES NEWS...

Freddie Goodwin was raging with referee Ivan Smith: "That referee cost us the match. I've no doubt about that." Billy Bremner finishes fifth in a vote for the best player in Europe. Don Revie plans to take two members of the staff to the World Cup in Germany next summer.

FIRST DIVISION HEADLINES...

Peter Cormack scores as Liverpool win 1-0 at Chelsea... Paul Fletcher equalises for Burnley, who are held 1-1 by Wolves... Joe Royle scores a penalty in Everton's 2-1 win over Derby... Frank Worthington scores in Leicester's 2-0 win over Arsenal... Brian Greenhoff scores in Stoke's 4-1 win over QPR.

FOOTBALL NEWS...

ITV scrap a feature about the FA Cup on New Year's Day because of a clash with a full Football League programme... Former England striker Jeff Astle is pleading with WBA boss Don Howe to let him leave... Stan Bowles admits he can't stop gambling and never sees his pay packet.

NEWS HEADLINES...

Joseph Sieff, the President of Marks and Spencer, survives an assassination attempt by the Popular Front for the Liberation of Palestine at his London home... Britain launch a trade drive to claw back all the extra money from dearer oil prices from Middle East countries... The Metropolitan Police arrest 170 people after a series of raids across London.

MATCH 24 - 1 January 1974

LEEDS 1
TOTTENHAM HOTSPUR 1

Attendance: 46,545

CHRIS McGRATH scored a 75th-minute equaliser after Bill Nicholson changed his mind about substituting him. McGrath took advantage of Gordon McQueen's 75th-minute mistake to slip the ball past David Harvey. Spurs had served notice of what was to come when Martin Peters tried a cunning 20-yard chip after four minutes. But Leeds took the lead through Mick Jones with their first shot on target after 18 minutes. Trevor Cherry hit the post, and Terry Naylor cleared a Paul Madeley effort off the line while Pat Jennings made brilliant stops from Madeley, Allan Clarke, Norman Hunter and Lorimer.

LEEDS David Harvey, Paul Reaney, Trevor Cherry, Billy Bremner, Gordon McQueen, Norman Hunter, Peter Lorimer, Allan Clarke (Terry Yorath), Mick Jones, Joe Jordan, Paul Madeley

SPURS: Pat Jennings, Ray Evans, Terry Naylor (Jimmy Neighbour), John Pratt, Mike England, Phil Beal, Mike Dillon, Steve Perryman, Martin Chivers, Martin Peters, Chris McGrath

Referee: R Mathewson

WHITES NEWS...

Leeds need a replay to beat Wolves in the FA Cup and draw Peterborough: "We learned our lesson at Colchester. Fourth Division sides are no pushovers in the FA Cup, especially when they are playing at home," said Deon Revie. Scotland boss Willie Ormond has asked Leeds if Gordon McQueen is available for two under-23 internationals.

FIRST DIVISION HEADLINES...

Peter Cormack scores as Liverpool are held 1-1 by Leicester City... David Cross equalises in Coventry's 1-1 draw with Burnley... Bryan Hamilton gets two goals for Ipswich, who beat Everton 3-1... Terry Hibbitt scores as Newcastle win 1-0 at Arsenal... Stan Bowles gets two as QPR beat Man Utd 3-0.

FOOTBALL NEWS...

Nearly 40,000 turn up to watch Bolton's 3-2 FA Cup win over Stoke as Sunday football gets underway... The FA fines Arsenal and England star Alan Ball £75 after describing English referees as 'a joke'... George Best goes missing again, and a showdown with Man Utd is on the cards.

NEWS HEADLINES...

Tax Ritter, the singing cowboy actor, dies of a heart attack while visiting a Nashville jail... 1,000 people sign on as temporary unemployed after the three day week starts... Lord Carrington is appointed the Government's new Energy Supremo... British Rail is on a collision course with unions over a plan to send home train drivers who refuse to work.

MATCH 25 - 12 January 1974

LEEDS 2
SOUTHAMPTON 1

Attendance: 35,000

MICK JONES and Joe Jordan were on target as Leeds took their unbeaten run to 25 games. Jones should have given Leeds a 15th-minute lead but had his third effort in a week disallowed for offside. Six minutes later, Jordan waltzed past Jim Steele on the right before crossing for Jones to apply the finish. Then, ten minutes after the break, Jones stabbed at Peter Lorimer's centre, and Jordan slammed the ball over the line. It was cruise control from then on, but Southampton pulled an 87th-minute goal back when Mick Channon stole in to head home Terry Paine's centre.

LEEDS David Harvey, Paul Reaney, Trevor Cherry, Billy Bremner, Paul Madeley, Norman Hunter, Peter Lorimer, Joe Jordan, Mick Jones, Terry Yorath, Frank Gray

SOUTHAMPTON: Eric Martin, Bob McCarthy, Steve Mills, Hugh Fisher, Paul Bennett, Jim Steele, Terry Paine, Mick Channon, Paul Gilchrist, Brian O'Neil, Ally McLeod (Bobby Stokes)

Referee: GW Hill

WHITES NEWS...

Terry Cooper makes his comeback for the reserves at Newcastle United after two years out with a broken leg suffered in an April 1972 clash with Stoke City's John Marsh. "I was terrified. I didn't know what to expect. I cannot wait to play in front of a packed Elland Road Kop again."

FIRST DIVISION HEADLINES...

Kevin Keegan scores two in Liverpool's 3-2 win over Birmingham... Kevin Hector's hat-trick helps Derby County hammer Burnley 5-1... Don Givens scores as QPR beat Everton 1-0... Geoff Hurst equalises for Stoke, who draw 1-1 at Ipswich... Billy Bonds late winner helps West Ham beat Man Utd 2-1.

FOOTBALL NEWS...

The Football League gives the go-ahead for games to be played on a Sunday during the energy crisis... Crystal Palace put full-back Tony Taylor on the transfer list after a dressing room punch-up with coach Frank Lord... England have been drawn in Group One of the Nations Cup against Czechoslovakia, Portugal and Cyprus.

NEWS HEADLINES...

Bing Crosby has part of a lung removed in an operation in San Francisco... Energy minister Lord Carrington has hinted at an increase in the three day week to four days... Prime Minister Ted Heath has postponed a decision about a snap general election in February...ASLEF have refused to lift the ban on train drivers working Sunday overtime and rest days.

MATCH 26 - 19 January 1974

EVERTON o
LEEDS o
Attendance: 55,740

LEEDS were held to a third draw in the last four games after failing to score for the first time since the end of November. Everton, only beaten once at home all season, gave Leeds a rough ride. They could have taken the lead after only 30 seconds when Paul Reaney and David Harvey failed to clear, but John Connolly blazed wide. Harvey then produced a brilliant save to keep out a Gary Jones' thunderbolt. Leeds were the better side after the break, and Everton needed David Lawson to keep them level, while Jones had late claims for a penalty rejected when he stumbled after a Mick Lyons tackle.

EVERTON: David Lawson, Terry Darracott, John McLaughlin, Dave Clements, Mike Lyons, John Hurst, Mike Bernard, Mick Buckley, Joe Royle, Gary Jones, John Connolly (Joe Harper)

LEEDS David Harvey, Paul Reaney, Trevor Cherry, Billy Bremner, Paul Madeley, Norman Hunter, Peter Lorimer, Joe Jordan, Mick Jones, Terry Yorath, Frank Gray (Roy Ellam)

Referee: RC Challis

WHITES NEWS...

Johnny Giles made his comeback to action after three months out of action in the reserves' 1-0 win against Bolton. Giles, who is recovering from a knee operation, played the whole of the second half, and Don Revie says he has an outside chance of facing Peterborough United in the FA Cup.

FIRST DIVISION HEADLINES...

Tommy Smith's last minute equaliser earns Liverpool a 1-1 draw with Stoke... A Tony Currie winner helps Sheffield Utd beat Burnley 2-1... Frank Worthington's hat-trick sees Leicester beat Ipswich 5-0... Jeff Bourne levels for Derby, who draw 1-1 at Chelsea... Mick Channon's brave header helps Southampton draw 2-2 with QPR.

FOOTBALL NEWS...

The Isthmian League is set to become the first to have no distinctions between amateurs and professionals from August... Swindon goalkeeper Jimmy Allan will refuse to play on a Sunday: "Sunday is for church and not football." The BBC are considering showing live matches from the continent on a Saturday afternoon with the domestic contract ending this season.

NEWS HEADLINES...

260,000 members of the minors union are preparing for a strike ballot... President Nixon believes it's time to end the Watergate investigation, and he has no plans to resign... The wholesale price of bacon and eggs has dropped which should mean cheaper breakfasts for millions. Bacon will be down to 48p per lb and eggs to 40p a dozen.

UK's No 1 Single: You Won't Find Another Fool Like Me ft Lyn Paul - The New Seekers

MATCH 27 - 2 February 1974

LEEDS 1
CHELSEA 1

Attendance: 41,520

DAVID HARVEY produced a stunning last-minute save to protect Leeds's 27-match unbeaten record. Harvey, who has been carrying an ankle injury, showed that there was nothing wrong with his hands, brilliantly stopping Chris Garland's cross-shot. Chelsea put Leeds's proud record in severe jeopardy and took the lead after 40 minutes when Bill Garner took advantage of Gordon McQueen's poor position to head home a John Hollins cross. Leeds launched wave after wave of attacks after the break and were rewarded after 67 minutes thanks to a brave Terry Cherry header from a Billy Bremner cross. John Phillips kept out Peter Lorimer before Harvey's heroics.

LEEDS David Harvey, Paul Reaney, Trevor Cherry, Billy Bremner, Gordon McQueen, Norman Hunter, Peter Lorimer, Allan Clarke, Joe Jordan, Terry Cooper (Terry Yorath), Paul Madeley

CHELSEA: John Phillips, Gary Locke, Ron Harris, John Hollins, Micky Droy, Dave Webb, Ian Britton, Chris Garland, Steve Kember, Bill Garner, Charlie Cooke

Referee: PG Reeves

WHITES NEWS...

Terry Cooper returned to the team for the win over Peterborough in the FA Cup and then made his first league appearance in 22 months in the hard fought draw against Chelsea before declaring: "It was just the type of game I needed. Another two, and I should just about be back."

FIRST DIVISION HEADLINES...

Peter Cormack scores as second placed Liverpool beat Norwich 1-0... Roy McFarland nets as Derby beat Newcastle 1-0... Liam Brady's own goal helps Burnley draw 1-1 at Arsenal... Trevor Whymark gets a brace as Ipswich thrash Southampton 7-0 at Portman Road... Leicester draw 0-0 at QPR.

FOOTBALL NEWS...

Football League clubs have rejected a new three-year television contract from the BBC and ITV... The Football League have given the green light for Sunday football to continue during the energy crisis after crowd figures rocketed... Southern League Tonbridge, who failed to sign George Best, are now trying to tempt Jimmy Greaves out of his two-year retirement.

NEWS HEADLINES...

Great Train Robber Ronnie Biggs, on the run since July 1965, is arrested in Rio de Janeiro, Brazil, by two Scotland Yard flying squad detectives... Eleven people are murdered when a coach-carrying serviceman and their families is blown up on the M62 in Yorkshire... 81 per cent of coal miners with the NUM have voted for a strike.

UK's No 1 Single: Tiger Feet - Mud

MATCH 28 - 5 February 1974

LEEDS 3
ARSENAL 1

Attendance: 26,778

JOE JORDAN scored twice in a three-goal, six-minute blitz as Leeds came from behind to extend their unbeaten record to 28 games. Peter Lorimer had missed a couple of chances before, in the 25th minute, Pat Rice and Sammy Nelson combined down the right before Alan Ball side-footed in from 14 yards. Bob Wilson produced a string of fine saves and looked to have Joe Jordan's header covered when Peter Simpson turned it into an own goal. Jordan headed Billy Bremner's cross in off the post in the 69th minute before Paul Madley robbed Arsenal at the kick-off, slipping him in to hit a hard shot past Wilson.

LEEDS David Harvey, Paul Reaney, Trevor Cherry, Billy Bremner, Roy Ellam, Norman Hunter, Peter Lorimer, Allan Clarke, Joe Jordan, Terry Yorath, Paul Madeley

ARSENAL: Bob Wilson, Pat Rice, Sammy Nelson, Peter Storey, Jeff Blockley, Peter Simpson, George Armstrong, Alan Ball, John Radford, Ray Kennedy, Liam Brady

Referee: E Jolly

WHITES NEWS...

Leeds have been given a clear hint that they will not have to pay the £3,000 suspended FA fine that has been hanging over their heads all season. Mick Jones is fit to return after missing three matches with a leg injury, and Gordon McQueen should be back to face Man Utd as well.

FIRST DIVISION HEADLINES...

Kevin Keegan gets Liverpool's second goal as they beat Coventry 2-1... Colin Bell scores as Man City see off Derby 1-0... Martin Chivers gets a hat-trick as Spurs beat Birmingham 4-2... John Benson nets as Norwich win 2-1 at QPR... Hugh Fisher scores in Southampton's 3-2 win over Newcastle.

FOOTBALL NEWS...

Former Leeds star Mike O'Grady is sacked by Rotherham for a breach of his contract... Wolves skipper Mike Bailey could miss the League Cup Final on March 2nd after breaking a toe...Brighton players are angry after manager Brian Clough tells them they are not fit to be footballers.

NEWS HEADLINES...

Parliament is dissolved ahead of the general election on February 28th... The 10.30 curfew on television programmes has been suspended to allow coverage of the election campaign...Leaders of the NUM reject a plea from Prime Minister Ted Heath for peace for the whole length of the general election campaign.

MATCH 29 - 9 February 1974

MANCHESTER UNITED 0
LEEDS 2

Attendance: 60,025

MICK JONES returned from injury to score his 14th league goal of the season as Leeds drove another nail into Manchester United's relegation coffin. Paul Madeley, Peter Lorimer and Allan Clarke all wasted chances to put the game out of reach before half-time while Brian Greenhoff cleared off his own line. Brian Kidd ripped in two shots that David Harvey saved as United kept biting away. Then on 57 minutes Madeley delivered a perfect centre for Jones to sweep past Alex Stepney. Joe Jordan had only been on the pitch for two minutes when he raced onto a superb 87th-minute Hunter pass to make the points safe.

MAN U: Alex Stepney, Martin Buchan, Stewart Houston, Brian Greenhoff, Jim Holton, Steve James, Willie Morgan, Lou Macari, Brian Kidd, Tony Young, Alex Forsyth (Sammy McIlroy)

LEEDS David Harvey, Paul Reaney (Joe Jordan), Trevor Cherry, Billy Bremner, Gordon McQueen, Norman Hunter, Peter Lorimer, Allan Clarke, Mick Jones, Terry Yorath, Paul Madeley

Referee: THC Reynolds

WHITES NEWS...

Leeds spared the blushes of ITV by allowing highlights of their FA Cup fifth-round replay defeat against Bristol City to be shown. An agreement was reached two hours before kick-off after QPR banned cameras. Gordon McQueen, Paul Reaney and Mick Jones are all on the treatment table.

FIRST DIVISION HEADLINES...

Peter Morris gets the Ipswich goal in the 1-0 win at Burnley... Mike Lyons scores as Everton beat Wolves 2-1... Clyde Best scores as West Ham win 1-0 at Leicester... Coventry score two own goals as they crash 5-1 at Newcastle... Dave Webb scores in Chelsea's 1-0 over Man City.

FOOTBALL NEWS...

The Football League have announced that average crowds are down by 315 to 12,528 citing early kick-offs and transport problems... Burnley are warned they could be banned from the FA Cup next season if they continue to ban television cameras from cup ties... Wales will follow England and Scotland by advertising for a full-time manager.

NEWS HEADLINES...

George Best is charged with theft of items from the home of current Miss World Marjorie Wallace... The latest polls suggest the Tories, on 41%, are .5% ahead of Labour... The Stock Exchange may stay open until 5pm instead of the current 3.30 pm under new proposals.

MATCH 30 - 23 February 1974

STOKE CITY 3
LEEDS 2

Attendance: 39,687

DENIS SMITH scored a dramatic winner as Leeds failed to equal Burnley's 53-year-old 30-match unbeaten record. It looked like it was going to be a routine win when Billy Bremner clipped home a quickly taken 14th-minute free-kick. Then, four minutes later, Allan Clarke added a second with a powerful shot. Mike Pejic got Stoke back into the game with a 20-yard free kick after 26 minutes, and eight minutes later, Alan Hudson equalised after John Ritchie picked him out in a packed area. The killer blow came in the 68th minute when Geoff Hurst's cross found Smith in heavy traffic, and his bullet header beat David Harvey.

STOKE: John Farmer, Jackie Marsh, Mike Pejic, Alan Dodd, Denis Smith, John Mahoney, Jimmy Robertson, Jimmy Greenhoff, Geoff Hurst, Alan Hudson, John Ritchie

LEEDS David Harvey, Terry Yorath, Trevor Cherry, Billy Bremner, Norman Hunter, Peter Lorimer, Allan Clarke, Joe Jordan, Johnny Giles (Terry Cooper), Paul Madeley

Referee: BJ Homewood

WHITES NEWS...

Referee John Holmwood slammed his dressing room door in the faces of Billy Bremner and Allan Clarke when they confronted him after the defeat at Stoke. They were angry after being booked by the Surrey official. Don Revie says that Leeds are now looking to wrap up the title.

FIRST DIVISION HEADLINES...

Liverpool are held to a 0-0 draw at Newcastle... Jeff Bourne gets a brace as Derby County win 4-2 at Norwich City... John Pratt equalises as Spurs draw 1-1 with Ipswich... John Hurst scores for Everton, who beat Coventry 1-0... Stan Bowles scores twice in QPR's 3-3 at Chelsea.

FOOTBALL NEWS...

Bill Shankly claims his Liverpool side, who are eight points behind Leeds, are ready to do the League and FA Cup double. The FA council postpone plans to end the distinction between amateurs and professionals until the 1975-76 season... Sir Alf Ramsey won't tour with the under-23 side in May because it clashes with the Home International Championship...

NEWS HEADLINES...

Former top BBC Raymond Glendenning has died at his Buckinghamshire home. He was 66... Enoch Powell, who is not seeking re-election, says standing for the Tories again would have caused his "moral and intellectual destruction".... Ivor Bell, the IRA's leader in Belfast, is captured by soldiers from the Devon and Dorset regiment.

UK's No 1 Single: Devil Gate Drive - Suzi Quatro

MATCH 31 - 26 February 1974

LEEDS 1
LEICESTER CITY 1

Attendance: 30,543

PETER LORIMER scored his first league goal since September but it wasn't enough to stop Leeds from again slipping up. Lorimer gave his side a 25th-minute lead from the penalty spot after Peter Shilton hauled down Joe Jordan as he chased Allan Clarke's overhead kick. Shilton kept Leicester in the game early on, palming a rising Billy Bremner shot over the bar and holding a 25-yard Roy Ellam shot. Non-stop second-half pressure from Leicester saw Len Glover have a shot kicked off the line by Paul Reaney. And they were rewarded in the 76th minute when Frank Worthington tapped the ball to Keith Weller, who beat David Stewart from eight yards.

LEEDS David Harvey, Paul Reaney, Trevor Cherry, Billy Bremner, Roy Ellam, Norman Hunter, Peter Lorimer, Allan Clarke, Joe Jordan, Terry Yorath (Frank Gray), Paul Madeley

LEICESTER: Peter Shilton, Steve Whitworth, Dennis Rofe, Steve Earle, Malcolm Munro, Graham Cross, Keith Weller, Jon Sammels, Frank Worthington, Alan Woolett, Len Glover

Referee: ED Wallace

WHITES NEWS...

Billy Bremner, Paul Madeley and Norman Hunter are on the short list of six for the PFA Player of the Year award. Bremner was a 3-1 favourite when betting closed. "Nobody wanted to back any of the other players, and we will lose if Billy gains the award", said a Ladbrokes spokesman.

FIRST DIVISION HEADLINES...

Dave Thomas scores for QPR, who beat Burnley 2-1... Dennis Mortimer's goal earns Coventry a 1-0 win over Norwich... Phil Boersma's late winner sees Liverpool beat Southampton 1-0... Mick Mills equalises for Ipswich, who draw 1-1 with Chelsea, who led through a Chris Garland strike.

FOOTBALL NEWS...

Man City will be on £2,500 to beat Wolves in the League Cup Final at Wembley... Chelsea boss Dave Sexton has transfer-listed Ian Hutchinson and suspended Tommy Baldwin for two weeks after missing training... The FA claims England's clash with Scotland at Hampden Park in May will be shown live on TV despite no contracts being signed.

NEWS HEADLINES...

Prime Minister Ted Heath is spending the weekend testing the support for a minority Tory Government after winning 296 seats against Labours 301... Miners Union President Joe Gormley raises hopes of a quick settlement to the dispute that has brought Britain to its knees... The Stock Market suffers a £300m crash market panic in a shock reaction to the election result.

MATCH 32 - 2 March 1974

LEEDS 1
NEWCASTLE UNITED 1

Attendance: 46,611

ALLAN CLARKE opened the scoring, but Leeds extended their winless run to three games. Newcastle looked the better team in the first half and were unlucky not to have taken the lead when Dave Stewart needed to make a brilliant save to keep out Malcolm MacDonald. Don Revie's side improved, and a minute after the break, Clarke won the ball back before squeezing a shot between Ian McFaul and the post. They were only ahead for five minutes however when Stewart Barrowclough held off a challenge to fire home past Stewart following a Norman Hunter mistake. Lorimer later blasted wide when clean through, and McFaul tipped over a powerful Trevor Cherry effort before Barrowclough missed an open goal.

LEEDS David Stewart, Paul Reaney, Trevor Cherry, Billy Bremner, Gordon McQueen, Norman Hunter, Peter Lorimer (Garry Liddell), Allan Clarke, Joe Jordan, Terry Yorath, Frank Gray

NEWCASTLE: Iam McFaul, David Craig, Alan Kennedy, Terry McDermott, Frank Clark, Bobby Moncur, Stewart Barrowclough, Tommy Cassidy, Malcolm McDonald, John Tudor, Jim Smith

Referee: C Thomas

WHITES NEWS...

Norman Hunter wins the PFA Player of the Year award. "This is the greatest honour I have ever received," he said. Hunter is named in the First Division team of the season along with Paul Madeley, Billy Bremner and Johnny Giles. Don Revie denies Madeley refused to play as a centre-half against Newcastle.

FIRST DIVISION HEADLINES...

John Toshack's last-minute goal sees Liverpool beat Burnley 1-0... John Ritchie's equaliser earns Stoke a 1-1 draw at Derby... Gerry Francis scores as QPR beat Spurs 3-1... Billy Bonds's hat-trick helps West Ham beat Chelsea 3-0... Phil Boyer equalises as Norwich draw 1-1 at arch-rivals Ipswich.

FOOTBALL NEWS...

Chelsea directors meet for six hours to discuss the future of manager Dave Sexton... Wolves win the League Cup after beating Man City 2-1 at Wembley... Glentoran's Roy Stewart dies of a heart attack two days after playing in a Cup Winners Cup quarter final against Borussia Monchengladbach.

NEWS HEADLINES...

Ted Heath resigns, and Harold Wilson becomes Prime Minister for a third time as Labour form a minority government, after the Liberals reject a Tory coalition... Miners agree on a pay rise of up to £16 while London Underground drivers and bank workers head a pay stampede... A 14% rise in the cost of living is predicted. The sharpest rise since 1940.

MATCH 33 - 9 March 1974

LEEDS 1
MANCHESTER CITY 0

Attendance: 37,578

JOHN HUNTING found himself at the centre of a cheating storm after awarding Leeds what turned out to be a match-winning penalty. The Leicestershire official decided in the 30th minute that Billy Bremner was fouled by Mike Doyle, sparking furious City protests which continued after Peter Lorimer sent Joe Corrigan the wrong way from the spot. Bremner had earlier seen Corrigan make two saves to keep him out. While for Leeds, Paul Madeley returned to the side after illness and controlled the midfield, and David Stewart, again standing in for the injured Harvey, handled everything City could throw at him in a confident style.

LEEDS David Stewart, Paul Reaney, Trevor Cherry, Billy Bremner, Gordon McQueen, Norman Hunter, Peter Lorimer, Allan Clarke, Joe Jordan, Terry Yorath, Paul Madeley

MAN C: Joe Corrigan, Glyn Pardoe, Willie Donachie, Mike Doyle, Tommy Booth, Tony Towers, Mike Summerbee, Colin Bell, Francis Lee, Denis Law, Rodney Marsh

Referee: J Hunting

WHITES NEWS...

Leeds have changed their away kit to all yellow and could wear it against Liverpool. Hull failed in a bid to sign Terry Cooper on loan for the rest of the season. David Harvey and Mick Jones could return at Anfield after missing the last three and four games respectively.

FIRST DIVISION HEADLINES...

Billy Bonds equalises to earn West Ham a 1-1 draw at Derby... Mike Lyons and Bob Latchford get braces in Everton's 4-1 win over Birmingham... Ted McDougall scores as Norwich draw 2-2 with Chelsea... Derek Dougan scores in Wolves 3-1 win over Ipswich.

FOOTBALL NEWS...

The FA order a replay of the riot-hit FA Cup quarter-final between Newcastle and Nottingham Forest... Fulham beat the transfer deadline to sign Bobby Moore from West Ham for £25,000... Referee Clive Thomas halts the Manchester derby for five minutes after Lou Macari and Mike Doyle refuse to leave the pitch after being sent off.

NEWS HEADLINES...

Building society chiefs are planning a meeting amid suggestions mortgages could rise by 2% to 13%... Prime Minister Ted Heath could call another general election if he is defeated in a vote on the Queen's Speech... British spies, brothers Kenneth and Keith Littlejohn, who claim they were recruited to infiltrate the IRA, escape from Dublin's maximum security Mountjoy jail...

UK's No. 1 Single: Jealous Mind - Alvin Stardust

MATCH 34 - 16 March 1974

LIVERPOOL 1
LEEDS 0

Attendance: 56,003

STEVE HIGHWAY blew the title race wide open after his 82nd-minute goal settled a pulsating match at Anfield. Don Revie, who was celebrating 13 years in charge at Elland Road, has only seen his side win one of the last seven games. They are six points clear at the top, but Liverpool have two games in hand. Norman Hunter cleared a John Toshack header off the line before Emlyn Hughes did the same for Liverpool after Peter Lorimer lobbed Ray Clemence. But just as it looked like Leeds were going to hold out for a point, Highway squeezed past Hunter and Trevor Cherry to toe-end the ball past David Harvey.

LIVERPOOL: Ray Clemence, Tommy Smith, Alec Lindsay, Phil Thompson, Peter McCormack, Emlyn Hughes, Kevin Keegan, Brian Hall, Steve Highway, John Toshack, Ian Callaghan

LEEDS David Harvey, Paul Reaney, Trevor Cherry, Billy Bremner, Gordon McQueen, Norman Hunter, Peter Lorimer, Allan Clarke, Joe Jordan (Mick Jones), Terry Yorath, Paul Madeley

Referee: JK Taylor

WHITES NEWS...

Leeds have unveiled an ambitious five-year £500,000 scheme to give Elland Road a facelift and turn it into one of the best in Europe. Leeds failed to agree terms with Man City to sign Mike Summerbee. Norman Hunter, Allan Clarke and Paul Madeley pull out of England training, much to the fury of Sir Alf Ramsey.

FIRST DIVISION HEADLINES...

Roy McFarland scores as Derby win 1-0 at Leicester... Peter Simpson equalises to earn Arsenal a 2-2 draw at Ipswich... QPR draw 0-0 with Wolves... John Ritchie scores a hat-trick in Stoke's 4-1 win over Southampton... Burnley score three times in as many minutes to beat Everton 3-1.

FOOTBALL NEWS...

Minister for Sport Denis Howell sets up a committee to study player discipline and crowd behaviour in football... The Football League beat the Scottish League 5-0, with Stan Bowles and Trevor Brooking among the goals... Scotland fans have snapped up almost 25,000 tickets for the World Cup Finals in West Germany this summer.

NEWS HEADLINES...

Princess Anne escapes uninjured after a £1m kidnap attempt in The Mall was foiled... Ted Heath faces a Tory leadership battle after the shadow cabinet refuse to vote on an amendment to the Queen's Speech... High Court Mr Justice Dunn has to apologise after claiming northern wives don't mind being beaten, but draw the line at adultery, while in the south, it's the opposite.

UK's No. 1 Single: Billy - Don't Be A Hero - Paper Lace

MATCH 35 - 23 March 1974

LEEDS 1
BURNLEY 4

Attendance: 39,453

PAUL FLETCHER inspired Cup finalists Burnley to send title-chasing Leeds spinning to their first home defeat of the season. The Whites started well, Peter Lorimer hitting the bar with Alan Stevenson beaten, before Fletcher opened the scoring on 17 minutes with a close-range finish after Frank Casper worked opening. Allan Clarke headed Leeds level after 39 minutes but their joy lasted less than a minute when Fletcher's overhead kick gave David Harvey no chance. Doug Collins chipped a neat lob over Harvey after 62 minutes before Geoff Nulty's close-range header rounded off the scoring seven minutes later.

LEEDS David Harvey, Paul Reaney, Trevor Cherry, Billy Bremner, Gordon McQueen, Norman Hunter, Peter Lorimer (Mick Jones), Allan Clarke, Joe Jordan, Terry Yorath, Paul Madeley

BURNLEY: Alan Stevenson, Peter Noble, Keith Newton, Martin Dobson, Colin Waldron, Jim Thomson, Geoff Nulty, Frank Casper, Paul Fletcher, Doug Collins (Billy Ingham), Leighton James

Referee: R Capey

WHITES NEWS...

Burnley's controversial chairman Bob Lord wasn't at Elland Road for a showdown with Leeds chairman Manny Cousins after his disparaging comments about Don Revie's side. Chief Scout Tony Collins has watched Bristol City's Gerry Gow for the ninth time this season. Collins took Gow to Ashton Gate from Glasgow Schools football.

FIRST DIVISION HEADLINES...

Brian Hall scores as Liverpool win 1-0 at Wolves... Kevin Hector is on target in Derby's 2-0 win over Ipswich... Gerry Francis' strike earns QPR a 1-0 win at Coventry... Bill Garner levels as Chelsea draw 1-1 at Everton... John Sissons scores two in Norwich's 4-0 win over Stoke.

FOOTBALL NEWS...

Sir Alf Ramsey ditches World Cup winners Bobby Moore and Alan Ball for England's trip to Portugal... Brian Lane, the manager of the pop group Yes, is offering to put £1m into Fourth Division strugglers Brentford... Bill Shankly hasn't taken his double-chasing Liverpool team away for special training ahead of their FA Cup semi-final against Leicester to keep preparations as normal as possible.

NEWS HEADLINES...

Chancellor Dennis Healey's budget raises tax by 3%, and the top rate is increased by 8p to 8.3p in the £. Prices of letters, telephones, rail fares, coal, electricity, petrol, cigarettes and alcohol will also increase... British spy Kenneth Littlejohn, who escaped from a Dublin jail three weeks ago, is back in Britain.

MATCH 36 - 30 Match 1974

WEST HAM UNITED 3
LEEDS 1

Attendance: 38,416

ALLAN CLARKE, banned for the next two games, put Leeds ahead before suffering a second-half meltdown. The Whites title chances could be slipping away after a third successive defeat, and Liverpool having three games in hand. They looked to be on their way to a routine win when he glanced home a Johnny Giles chipped pass. Clyde Best raced clear after 50 minutes to pull a goal back. The turning point came soon afterwards when referee John Yates changed his mind and disallowed another Clarke goal. It knocked the stuffing out of Leeds. Pop Robson beat Harvey with a 61st-minute bullet header before Brooking made it safe in the 84th minute.

WEST HAM: Mervyn Day, Keith Coleman, Frank Lampard, Billy Bonds, Tommy Taylor, Mick McGiven, John McDowell, Graham Paddon, Pop Robson, Trevor Brooking, Clyde Best

LEEDS David Harvey, Paul Reaney, Trevor Cherry, Billy Bremner, Gordon McQueen, Norman Hunter, Johnny Giles, Allan Clarke, Joe Jordan (Mick Jones), Terry Yorath, Paul Madeley

Referee: JH Yates

WHITES NEWS...

Allan Clarke was raging after the defeat at West Ham: "There is no way they are going to let us win." Long-term injury victims Eddie Gray and Mick Bates come back for the reserves. Don Revie is building a £40,000 canteen at Elland Road. "It's vital for the players to get the best steak and vegetables every day."

FIRST DIVISION HEADLINES...

Derby are held 0-0 at QPR while Stoke and Arsenal play out the same scoreline... Brian Talbot scores twice in Ipswich's 3-0 win over Coventry... Sammy McIlroy scores as Man Utd win 3-1 at Chelsea... John Connolly scores in Everton's 2-0 win at Spurs.

FOOTBALL NEWS...

Denis Law rejects a move to Ian St John's Motherwell because he doesn't want to leave the Manchester area... A new-look England side, with six new caps, draw 0-0 with Portugal in Lisbon... Exeter face a fine after refusing to play Scunthorpe because only nine of their 19 players are fit.

NEWS HEADLINES...

Britain's demands for better Common Market membership terms have received a cool reception from the eight other members... Industry Secretary Tony Benn has denied reports that the Concorde project is close to being cancelled... A former nun, Patrica Cairns, is jailed for six years after plotting to help Moors Murderer Myra Hindley escape from prison.

MATCH 37 - 6 April 1974

LEEDS 2
DERBY COUNTY 0

Attendance: 37,838

PETER LORIMER returned from the sidelines to score his first goal from open play since September as Leeds got their title challenge back on track. Derby had made the early running, David Harvey saving from David Nish and Kevin Hector, while Joe Jordan fired wide when clean through. But Lorimer, who was dropped at West Ham, made them pay, cooly lobbing Colin Boulton to give his side a 16th-minute lead. They doubled their advantage after 69 minutes when Billy Bremner netted from Trevor Cherry's free kick. Leeds should have had a late penalty when Lorimer was the victim of a dubious Peter Daniel tackle.

LEEDS David Harvey, Paul Reaney, Trevor Cherry, Billy Bremner, Gordon McQueen, Norman Hunter, Peter Lorimer, Johnny Giles, Joe Jordan, Terry Yorath, Paul Madeley

DERBY: Colin Boulton, Ron Webster, David Nish, Bruce Rioch (Alan Hinton), Peter Daniel, Colin Todd, Steve Powell, Archie Gemmill, Roger Davies, Kevin Hector, Jeff Bourne

Referee: JD Williams

WHITES NEWS...

Don Revie was delighted with the win over Derby: "After three defeats, this win can do wonders for us." Meanwhile the club have given free transfers to four reserve team players. Nigel Davey, John Shaw, Sean O'Neill and Jimmy Mann. Leeds, Derby and Man Utd have all scouted Watford marksman Bill Jennings.

FIRST DIVISION HEADLINES...

Dave Thomas scores for QPR, who lose 2-1 at Liverpool... Peter Morris scores for Ipswich, who beat Man City 3-1... Malcolm MacDonald nets twice as Newcastle beat Everton 2-1... John Ritchie scores twice in Stoke's 4-0 win over Burnley... Brian Greenhoff scores as Man Utd win 2-0 at Norwich.

FOOTBALL NEWS...

Frank O'Farrell accepts £40,000 to manage Iran's national team but stays with Cardiff until May... Newcastle and Liverpool are asking the FA to change their minds about scrapping extra time if the FA Cup Final ends in a draw... Pauline Baldwin, the ex-wife of Chelsea's Tommy Baldwin, is gagged by the Hugh Court from talking to newspapers about their marriage.

NEWS HEADLINES...

The IRA and its supporters firebomb and hijack public transport in Belfast... Prime Minister Harold Wilson calms Labour MPs over his alleged land deals, they feel newspapers had inflated claims... The Tory Monday Club has slammed the government amnesty for around 29,000 illegal immigrants from Commonwealth countries and Pakistan.

UK's No 1 Single: Seasons in The Sun - Terry Jacks

MATCH 38 - 13 April 1974

COVENTRY CITY o
LEEDS o

Attendance: 35,206

LEEDS took another small step towards the Championship title with a hard-fought point at Highfield Road. They travelled to the Midlands missing Allan Clarke and Mick Jones and clearly lacked sting, pushing Billy Bremner to partner Joe Jordan, and they didn't have a single clearcut chance. They were fortunate that Coventry also lacked any sort of finishing power despite having the better of the chances. David Cross twice fluffed his lines to score and earn his side a rare victory over the league leaders. Gordon McQueen was Leeds' biggest threat but saw Jimmy Holmes clear a header, and Dennis Mortimer, who had a header tipped over, charged down a shot.

COVENTRY: Bill Glazier, Wilf Smith, Jimmy Holmes, Dennis Mortimer, Peter Hindley, Alan Dugdale, John Craven, Brian Anderson, David Cross, Mick McGuire, Tommy Hutchinson

LEEDS David Harvey, Paul Reaney, Trevor Cherry, Billy Bremner, Gordon McQueen, Norman Hunter, Peter Lorimer, Terry Yorath, Joe Jordan, Johnny Giles, Paul Madeley

Referee: DW Smith

WHITES NEWS...

Mick Jones is fighting to overcome a knec injury, but Eddie Gray and Mick Bates are back in the squad. Middlesbrough boss Jack Charlton wants Johnny Giles to replace Bobby Murdoch. Charlton believes he can get his man for a £25,000 deal. Leeds, Chelsea, Everton, Millwall and Spurs watch Partick Thistle goalkeeper Alan Rough.

FIRST DIVISION HEADLINES...

Emlyn Hughes equalises for Liverpool in a 1-1 draw at Ipswich... Kevin Hector scores a hat-trick as Derby beat Sheffield Utd 4-1... Burnley draw 0-0 with Leicester... Bob Latchford scores in Everton's 4-1 win over Norwich City... Ray Kennedy scores twice as Arsenal win 3-1 at Chelsea.

FOOTBALL NEWS...

Newcastle boss Joe Harvey is threatening to play the reserves in the FA Cup Final after relegation-threatened Man Utd beat them... Easter Saturday Football League crowds were 541,633, down 20,683 from last season... A proposal to end traditional bonuses of £4 a win and £2 a draw has been blessed by a Football League committee.

NEWS HEADLINES...

Enoch Powell, who stood down at the General Election, says he is no longer a member of the Conservative Party... David Bowie has been voted top female vocalist in a BBC poll after World Service listeners mistake him for a woman... A transport company is being sued after 1,500,000 Oxo cubes weighing 28 tonnes and worth £13,000 go missing from a Dagenham, Essex warehouse.

MATCH 39 - 15 April 1974

LEEDS o
SHEFFIELD UNITED o

Attendance: 41,140

SWANSEA REFEREE Tom Reynolds needed a police escort after disallowing two goals to bring back memories of Ray Tinkler, costing Leeds the league title against WBA three years earlier. Reynolds also booked Norman Hunter, Trevor Cherry and Peter Lorimer before police reinforcements were brought in to protect the tunnel as events turned ugly. Mick Jones, back in the side after two months out, had a 51st-minute goal disallowed for offside before 14 minutes later, Peter Lorimer lashed home a powerful shot before Jim Brown could move. Reynolds ruled that Allan Clarke, back in the side after suspension, was offside, much to Leeds's fury.

LEEDS David Harvey, Paul Reaney, Trevor Cherry, Billy Bremner, Gordon McQueen, Norman Hunter, Peter Lorimer, Allan Clarke, Mick Jones, Johnny Giles (Frank Gray), Paul Madeley

SHEFF U: Jim Brown, Len Badger, Ted Hemsley, Keith Eddy, Eddie Colquhoun, Geoff Salmons, Alan Woodward, John Flynn, Terry Nicholl, Mick Speight, Tony Field

Referee: THC Reynolds

WHITES NEWS...

Norman Hunter has damaged a thigh, and Billy Bremner has a leg injury. Both face late fitness tests. Joe Jordan is out, while Dave Harvey who was struck in the eye by Mick Jones before the game, is fit. Leeds will visit Aston Villa on August 7 to mark the Midland side's centenary.

FIRST DIVISION HEADLINES...

David Johnson scores as Ipswich beat QPR 1-0... Kevin Hector is on target in Derby's 1-0 win over Coventry... Jim McCalliog scores twice as Man Utd beat Everton 3-0... Alan Sunderland scores two as Wolves beat Arsenal 3-1... Newcastle draw 0-0 with Norwich... Chelsea and Spurs share a goalless draw.

FOOTBALL NEWS...

Alan Ball says he doesn't want to leave Arsenal after being linked with a swap for Man Utd's Martin Buchan... Southampton boss Lawrie McMenemy says the relegation-threatened club won't see the best of £285,000 this season... Joao Havelange, who is running to be FIFA President, says it is time for Britain to lose its influence on the leadership of world football.

NEWS HEADLINES...

IRA's leading gunman in Ulster, Ivor Bell, escapes from the Maze Prison after swapping places with a prisoner due to be paroled... 18m households face an automatic rise in electricity prices in line with the increase in power station costs... TUC chiefs have sent out a 'go easy on pay' message to union barons.

MATCH 40 - 16 April 1974

SHEFFIELD UNITED 0
LEEDS 2

Attendance: 39,972

PETER LORIMER scored two of Leeds's most important goals of the season to put them within touching distance of their second Football League title in five years. It was only Leeds' third win in the last 11 games, but keeps them four points clear of Liverpool. Leeds could have made it more comfortable, but Terry Yorath fluffed a third-minute shot with only the keeper to beat after Mick Jones set him up. Leeds edged ahead after 58 minutes, John Flynn flicking Jones's header off the line only for Lorimer to crack home from an acute angle. Eleven minutes later, Jones was pushed by Mick Speight, and Lorimer confidently cracked home the penalty.

SHEFF U: Jim Brown, Len Badger, Ted Hemsley, Keith Eddy, Eddie Colquhoun, Geoff Salmons, Alan Woodward, John Flynn, Terry Nicholl, Mick Speight, Tony Field

LEEDS David Harvey, Paul Reaney, Trevor Cherry, Billy Bremner, Gordon McQueen, Norman Hunter, Peter Lorimer, Allan Clarke (Frank Gray), Mick Jones, Terry Yorath, Paul Madeley

Referee: AWS Jones

WHITES NEWS...

Mick Jones is having treatment for a knee injury ahead of the top-of-the-table clash with Ipswich. England boss Sir Alf Ramsey has dumped Allan Clarke for the British Championship, but Paul Madeley and Norman Hunter are recalled. Leeds have received 6,250 tickers for their match at QPR on Saturday week.

FIRST DIVISION HEADLINES...

Brian Hall scores twice as Liverpool beat Man City 4-0... Phil Boersma and Kevin Keegan are also on target... Geoff Hurst scores for Stoke, who draw 1-1 at Leicester... Bob Hatton scores twice as Birmingham draw 2-2 with Burnley... Ted McDougall scores for Norwich, who draw 1-1 with Newcastle.

FOOTBALL NEWS...

Atletico Madrid have six players banned by UEFA after their European Cup semi-final second leg against Celtic... Arsenal goalkeeper Bob Wilson confirmed he is retiring to join the BBC Sports Unit... Southern League referee John McCree is taken to hospital after being attacked by 100 Dartford fans following a 3-1 defeat to Maidstone Utd.

NEWS HEADLINES...

Kenneth Lennon, shot dead in Surrey, left a note claiming he was forced into informing for Special Branch on the IRA... 12,000 workers at the Austin Morris car plant in Oxford have been laid off because of a strike by transport drivers... The CBI says it would be madness for Britain to leave the Common Market despite demands for changes to EEC Policies

MATCH 41 - 20 April 1974

LEEDS 3
IPSWICH TOWN 2

Attendance: 44,015

ALLAN CLARKE netted the winner as Leeds marched to within a point of the title despite Ipswich coming back from two goals down. They will only need a point at QPR after Clarke forced home Paul Reaney's 69th-minute cross. Victory appeared a formality after Peter Lorimer opened the scoring after 15 minutes with a long-range screamer. And then seven minutes later, Paul Cooper couldn't hold Lorimer's thunderous free kick and Billy Bremner scored from the rebound. Brian Talbot gave David Harvey no chance from close range after 27 minutes, before Ipswich equalised in the 54th minute when Bryan Hamilton got a delicate touch on a Mick Mills cross, but Clarke and Leeds weren't to be denied.

LEEDS David Harvey, Paul Reaney, Trevor Cherry, Billy Bremner, Gordon McQueen, Norman Hunter, Peter Lorimer, Allan Clarke, Mick Jones, Paul Madeley, Eddie Gray

IPSWICH: Paul Cooper, George Burley, Mick Mills, Peter Morris, Allan Hunter, Kevin Beattie, Bryan Hamilton, Brian Talbot, David Johnson, Roger Osborne, Clive Woods

Referee: KW Baker

WHITES NEWS...

Terry Yorath admits he can't wait in the reserves for much longer: "I'll have to start thinking seriously about my future if things don't happen for me soon." Don Revie admits fining players has seen a 50 per cent improvement in bookings: "I hope we can do even better next season," he said.

FIRST DIVISION HEADLINES...

Liverpool draw 0-0 with Everton... Charlie George is on target for Arsenal, who beat Derby 2-0... Ted McDougall scores as Norwich beat Burnley 1-0... Sean Haslegrave scores for Stoke, who beat Spurs 1-0... Frank Worthington gets two in Leicester's 3-0 win over Chelsea.

FOOTBALL NEWS...

Newcastle will play all FA Cup ties next season away from St James Park after a riot in their quarter-final win over Nottingham Forest... The Football League vote to reject a £3.5m TV contract from BBC and Independent Television, raising the prospect of a black-out... Tottenham beat Lokomotive Leipzig to reach their second UEFA Cup Final.

NEWS HEADLINES...

Unions will be refunded £10m they paid in tax after refusing to register under the Industrial Relations Act... A demonstration by 250 wives of laid-off British Leyland workers turns violent when they attack a former Union official... Defence Secretary Roy Mason says British troops will stay in Ulster for as long as they are needed.

MATCH 42 - 27 April 1974

QUEENS PARK RANGERS 0
LEEDS 1

Attendance: 35,353

ALLAN CLARKE put the icing on top of the celebration cake with the only goal of the game in west London. Don Revie's side were crowned champions when Arsenal beat Liverpool in midweek but wanted to go out in style. Billy Bremner and Johnny Giles gave Rangers a first-half grilling while Gerry Francis and Dave Thomas pulled the strings for the home side, who could have been ahead, but David Harvey made superb saves from Stan Bowles and Terry Mancini. Clarke scored the only goal after 56 minutes after Joe Jordan placed a fine through ball between two defenders.

QPR: Phil Parkes, Martyn Busby, Ian Gillard, Terry Venables, Terry Mancini, Tony Hazell, Dave Thomas, Gerry Francis, Mick Leach, Stan Bowles, Don Givens

LEEDS David Harvey, Paul Reaney (Terry Yorath), Trevor Cherry, Billy Bremner, Gordon McQueen, Norman Hunter, Peter Lorimer, Allan Clarke, Joe Jordan, Johnny Giles, Paul Madeley

Referee: GW Hill

WHITES NEWS...

Billy Bremner, David Harvey, Peter Lorimer, Joe Jordan and Gordon McQueen are all named in Scotland's 40-man World Cup squad. Jimmy Mann joins Bristol City after being given a free transfer. York and Oldham wanted to speak to him. Leeds lost 2-0 to Huddersfield Town in the West Riding Cup.

FIRST DIVISION HEADLINES...

Kevin Keegan's last-minute equaliser earns Liverpool a 2-2 draw at West Ham... Steve Powell scores in Derby's 2-0 win over Wolves... Alan Woodward scores as Sheffield Utd beat Ipswich 1-0... Paul Fletcher nets in Burnley's 1-1 draw with Newcastle... John Radford's late equaliser earns Arsenal 3-3 at Coventry.

FOOTBALL NEWS...

Sir Alf Ramsey is sacked as England boss, and Joe Mercer is put in caretaker charge... Liverpool beat Newcastle 3-0 in the FA Cup Final at Wembley. Kevin Keegan scores twice, Steve Heighway gets the other... World Cup winner Alan Ball breaks a leg and could miss seven internationals, spelling the end of his international career.

NEWS HEADLINES...

IRA chief Ivor Bell, who escaped from the Maze Prison, is recaptured in a middle-class Protestant area... Burmah Oil and ICI announce plans to invest £600m to develop North Sea oilfields and a new chemical works... Police fear 5,000 'superb' forged £1 tickets for the FA Cup were in circulation ahead of the final, with a detective in charge saying they are the best he has come across.

PLAYER PROFILES

Mick Bates

A midfielder who made almost 200 appearances in 12 years at Elland Road, twice winning the Fairs Cup and the FA Cup, settled in Bentley near Doncaster, where he ran an insurance business for 21 years until retiring at the age of 52. He died in July 2021, aged 73.

Billy Bremner

Scottish international midfield enforcer. Don Revie's captain, also skippered his country at the 1974 World Cup Finals. He won six major trophies with Leeds and managed the club on either side of spells with Doncaster. He worked the after-dinner circuit before his death from a heart attack in December 1997, aged 54.

Trevor Cherry

England left-back made 486 appearances and scored 32 goals, taking over as captain from Billy Bremner. After managing Bradford City, Cherry became a successful businessman in promotions and hospitality, waste paper, a five-a-side football centre and property before his sudden death in April 2020, aged 72.

Allan Clarke

England striker was one of five footballing brothers. He scored 151 goals in 366 games for The Whites, winning the League Championship, FA Cup and Fairs Cup. Clarke managed Barnsley, Leeds, Scunthorpe and Lincoln before becoming a salesman at Wakefield-based MTS Nationwide until he retired aged 61, settling in Scunthorpe.

Terry Cooper

England left-back played in the 1970 World Cup quarter-finals and twice won the Fairs Cup. He managed Bristol Rovers, Bristol City, Exeter and Birmingham and was Southampton's European scout before retiring to the Canary Islands. His son Mark was a footballer and manager. Cooper died in July 2021, aged 77.

Roy Ellam

A central defender who won a Division Two Championship with Huddersfield but found his chances limited in his two seasons after his shock move to Elland Road, making just 21 appearances. He sold compost prior to running a couple of pubs and later worked in his daughter's fitness centre.

Johnny Giles

Republic of Ireland winger won two League titles, two Fairs Cups, an FA Cup and a League Cup after his bargain £33,000 move from Manchester United. He twice managed WBA and also took charge of theIreland, Shamrock Rovers and Vancouver Whitecaps before becoming a journalist and pundit in his native Dublin.

Eddie Gray

Scottish winger who won two Fairs Cups, making over 450 appearances, and played alongside his brother Frank at Elland Road. He managed Leeds, Rochdale and Hull City, has also run soccer camps, and worked in the media. Gray now works as a club ambassador, and his great-nephew Archie plays for Leeds.

Frank Gray

Scottish left-back won a European Cup with Nottingham Forest in between two spells at Elland Road. The younger brother of Eddie, went into management, coaching and scouting and has worked for Fox Sports Australia before returning to live on the South Coast. His son Andy and grandson Archie have played for Leeds.

David Harvey

Scottish international goalkeeper played in three FA Cup finals but missed the 1975 final following a car crash. He ran a pub, delivered fruit and veg, and was a postman in Yorkshire and then the Orkney Islands, where he also farmed. Harvey relocated to Lochmaben in Dumfries after retiring.

Norman Hunter

The England defender was an apprentice electrical fitter before joining the Leeds groundstaff, making 726 appearances and scoring 21 goals. The first PFA Player of the Year, he managed Barnsley and Rotherham before he sold sports goods and insurance and worked as a radio pundit. Hunter died from Covid-19 in April 2020.

Mick Jones

England forward who won two League Championship titles, two Fairs Cups and an FA Cup before being forced to retire with a knee injury. He became a sports goods rep before opening a sports shop then and then ran a Worksop market stall and later worked in corporate hospitality at Leeds.

Joe Jordan

Scotland international was a Cup Winners Cup and a European Cup finalist. He won Serie B honours with Milan, managed Bristol City, Hearts and Stoke, and then worked for a series of clubs under Harry Redknapp. He has been assistant manager at Middlesbrough and then coached at AFC Bournemouth.

Garry Liddell

A forward who was very much on the fringes at Elland Road with one goal in seven appearances. He helped Grimsby Town win promotions from Divisions Three and Four. He became an executive officer with the Employment Tribunal Service in Leeds but died in Stirling in April 2015. His son Andy was a footballer.

Peter Lorimer

Scottish international midfielder was the club's youngest-ever player and record goal scorer with 238 goals in over 700 appearances. A European Cup Finalist, he became the landlord of the Commercial Inn near Elland Road and worked as a media pundit and club ambassador. Lorimer died in March 2021 after a long battle with illness.

Paul Madeley

England international utility man who won two League titles and played in every outfield position for Leeds. He also helped the club win a Second Division title and, after retiring, went to work for the family business who had a chain of DIY stores, and later became a property consultant. He died in July 2018.

Gordon McQueen

The Scottish international defender was signed as Jack Charlton's replacement. He moved to Manchester United for a British record fee of £495,000. Managed Airdrie, and coached at Middlesbrough. Settled in North Yorkshire, he worked in the media and died in June 2023 after a battle with dementia. His daughter Hayley is a Sky Sports presenter.

Paul Reaney

England right-back who helped Leeds win promotion from Division Two and was part of the side that won seven major trophies in 16 seasons at Elland Road. Only Jack Charlton and Billy Bremner made more appearances. Reaney settled near Knaresborough, Yorkshire, running coaching courses at holiday camps and then owned a portrait company.

David Stewart

Scotland goalkeeper signed to replace Gary Sprake to understudy David Harvey. He started the European Cup final defeat to Bayern Munich and helped Swansea win promotion to Division One. After retiring, Stewart installed carpets and worked as a sales rep before becoming a goldsmith. He died in November 2018.

Terry Yorath

A Wales international midfielder who spent much of his time at Elland Road understudying Billy Bremner and Johnny Giles. A European Cup finalist, managed Swansea (twice), Wales, Bradford, Sheffield Wednesday, Cardiff, Lebanon and Margate, and he now lives in Leeds. He is the father of television presenter Gabby Logan.

The Manager
Don Revie

One of the greatest managers in British football history went on to manage England before leaving to take charge of the United Arab Emirates and club sides Al-Nasr and Al Ahly. Revie died in an Edinburgh hospital in May 1989, aged 61, after a battle with motor neurone disease.

Football League Division One 1973/74

		PLD	W	D	L	F	A	PTS
1	*LEEDS*	*42*	*24*	*14*	*4*	*66*	*31*	*62*
2	Liverpool	42	22	13	7	52	31	57
3	Derby County	42	17	14	11	52	42	48
4	Ipswich Town	42	18	11	13	67	58	47
5	Stoke City	42	15	16	11	54	42	46
6	Burnley	42	16	14	12	56	53	46
7	Everton	42	16	12	14	50	48	44
8	QPR	42	13	17	12	56	52	43
9	Leicester City	42	13	16	13	51	41	42
10	Arsenal	42	14	14	14	49	51	42
11	Tottenham Hotspur	42	14	14	14	45	50	42
12	Wolves	42	13	15	14	49	49	13
13	Sheffield United	42	14	12	16	44	49	40
14	Manchester City	42	14	12	16	39	46	40
15	Newcastle United	42	13	12	17	49	48	38
16	Coventry City	42	14	10	18	43	54	38
17	Chelsea	42	12	13	17	56	60	37
18	West Ham United	42	11	15	16	55	60	37
19	Birmingham City	42	12	13	17	52	64	37
20	Southampton	42	11	14	17	47	68	36
21	Manchester United	42	10	12	20	38	48	32
22	Norwich City	42	7	15	20	37	62	29

Appearances & Goals

	FULL	SUB	GOALS
David Harvey	48	0	0
David Stewart	4	0	0
John Shaw	1	0	0
Glan Letheran	0	1	0
Gary Sprake	1	0	0
Paul Reaney	44	0	0
Trevor Cherry	49	1	2
Frank Gray	9	4	1
Norman Hunter	49	0	0
Gordon McQueen	42	0	0
Paul Madeley	47	0	2
Roy Ellam	10	3	0
Sean O'Neill	0	2	0
Terry Cooper	3	1	0
Peter Hampton	1	0	0
Billy Bremner	52	0	11
Mick Bates	14	1	3
Peter Lorimer	47	0	14
Terry Yorath	33	5	3
John Giles	19	0	2
Eddie Gray	9	0	0
Joe Jordan	32	9	9
Allan Clarke	41	1	16
Mick Jones	36	3	17
Gary Liddell	2	2	1
Jimmy Mann	1	0	0
O.G.			1
TOTAL GOALS			**82**

Also available from Victor Publishing....

The 1980s are remembered as a bleak time in the history of English football. Dismissed as a time the game was blighted by hooliganism and tragedy. Since the advent of the Premier League in 1992, it's easy to forget that going to the match before then was still a hugely enjoyable experience, accessible and affordable to all. With new, modern, often soulless, identikit stadiums now commonplace, also forgotten are the unique stands, terraces, facades and features that gave every club its own identity. This book unearths a huge, previously unseen treasure trove of images from that forgotten era. An era that was, until now, lost.

Got a book in you?

PUBLISHING
victorpublishing.co.uk

This book is published by Victor Publishing.

Victor Publishing specialises in getting new and independent writers' work published worldwide in both paperback and Kindle format.
If you have a manuscript for a book of any genre (fiction, non-fiction, autobiographical, biographical or even reference or photographic/illustrative) and would like more information on how you can get your work published and on sale to the general public, please visit us at:
www.victorpublishing.co.uk

Printed in Great Britain
by Amazon

39206624R00059